Deep Calls Unto Deep

Dear Jeni,

I hope you will feel a deep satisfaction in the Deep calls unto Deep book. Only a few of us know of your substantial contribution to the work, but it will certainly matter as it makes its way into the world's readership.

Cordially,
Steve J. Van der Weele

2/17/15

Deep Calls Unto Deep

Images of God's Bounty and Man's Response

Arjan Plaisier

Secretary General of the
Protestant Church
of the Netherlands

Translated by

Steve J. Van der Weele

Calvin College
Grand Rapids, Michigan
2014

Translation of

Overvloed and Overgave
Een Caleidoscopisch Geloofsboek

Published by

Uitgeverij Boekcentrum,

Zoetermeer, The Netherlands
2013

WIPF & STOCK · Eugene, Oregon

This effort is dedicated to all adherents of the faith, but especially to those who have at least temporarily permitted other priorities to relegate faith matters to a subordinate role in their lives.

The way back is available to everyone, and it begins
at each person's front door.
—ARJAN PLASIER

I intend also with this book to honor the memory of my wife, Viola, and son-in-law Robert Kula, and to thank the other members of my family, daughter Deborah Renee, son Philip and his wife Joan, and two lovely granddaughters, Kathryn Ann and Jennifer Joy, for their role in my life.
—STEVE VAN DER WEELE

I am indebted to Sierd Woudstra, friend and colleague, for monitoring my translation, and to Jeni Hoekstra for her invaluable technical assistance.

Contents

Contents

Foreword

THE TITLE OF THIS book, *Overvloed and Overgave: Een caleidoscopisch geloofsboek* (Generosity and response: A kaleidoscopic devotional book) is high-spirited. Abundance is like an overflowing cup, like a waterfall that keeps running, like myriads of blooming flowers in spring, and like a waving field of grain ripe for harvesting. Surrender implies letting go of oneself; it is like jumping into the water and into opening arms. These may seem big words. But I have chosen the title with care, and I believe it is right for this book. Unfortunately, faith has become a minimalist affair. God has become a disappearing point on the horizon, and belief an embarrassment. The Christian tradition is seen as a relic from the past, and church a habit for which one must offer apologies and a polite assurance that he will not become intolerant. On the other hand, it happens too that faith can be made to appear like a ready-made package, a set of truths derived from an authoritative Bible, devoid of joy and freedom. This book is meant to counteract such mindsets. That is not the only reason I do so—and not the first reason. The primary motive derives from a deep love, and a passion. It is a declaration of affection for the unbounded generosity of God and, as such, a plea for belief as an appropriate response.

This exuberant generosity flows from God. He created the world from his own deep pulsating life. The creation which resulted from that life vibrates until this very day. What is more, God's relationship to his original creation and the original creation of man is one of overflowing good. It is a gift which extends beyond the understanding of what one might suppose possible and the heart can imagine. It is only through this burgeoning energy that life is possible for man. It is only through this pulsating life that there is more than can be supposed from the givens of the world, numbering our years, more than living with austerity, and more than deliberating over crises. Everywhere there is surplus, an increasingly more, an excess that comes to us through the grace and kindness of God.

This abundance persists even in times when this is no longer believed or acknowledged. Even so, this generosity begs for a response. What is given out of passionate generosity can be returned with passion. Where kindness and love streams out of heaven, there arises on the earth opportunity and freedom to reflect the divine opulence. Gift deserves reciprocity. Belief is not a timid nod, a calculating, "Yes, we know," a wrinkled forehead in advance, or a fanatical confrontation. Belief is the corresponding answer to bounty. All this began with Jesus and the apostles. And so it will continue, until the end of time.

The subtitle of the book is *A Kaleidoscopic Devotional*. A kaleidoscope is a tube-like container in which with great ingenuity colored bits of glass reflected by mirrors create pleasing patterns for the spectator when the instrument is rotated. In a similar way, in a manner of speaking, I have sought to do that in this book. It is a book of reflections and symbols. I activate the instrument three times and I receive four images.

I begin with God, as he has revealed himself to us. Four images characterize the nature of that revelation. They are embodied in the epic, the lyric, the dramatic, and the didactic. Literary categories, though not so much a description of God from the outside, can serve, as it will become apparent, to help us understand our life in the world in the light of God's revelation. How does your life look to you, and what difference does it make with a life outside of God's revelation?

In the second section I concern myself with faith. I won't attempt a definition of belief, but, rather, show how "flesh and blood" faith is present in today's people. For that I use the imagery of the seasons, giving attention to the spring, summer, autumn, and the winter manifestations of belief. These images give me a chance to engage in a conversation about faith formation as we encounter it in our culture.

In the third round, I deal with the church. Everyone is for spirituality, but there is no substitute for the church. Is the church, meanwhile, not being ignored as outdated, or falsified? I think not. The question is really what the church is and what you will find there. That is not wholly clear—not for church people either. For this subject I use four images of institutions—institutions well known—and I shall point out resemblances. It is about hospitals, the theater, parliament, and the temple.

Finally, for good measure, I propose yet another topic—this time on this idea, *the definition of reality*. What do people regard as *real* in the world we are living in? This time we introduce three traditional, highly respectable terms which, on close examination, still are very much alive. The terms are truth, goodness, and beauty. Of course, these are not images, but as it will appear, these terms can certainly call up all sorts of images.

We have now concluded our look into the kaleidoscope. That has revealed a great deal of material. But not too much either. Much more can still be said and heard.

You will not find that in this book. It is not intended as a comprehensive devotional. What I have written I have been led to write out of a *sense of urgency*. Here is what I wanted to say. The advantage of doing so is that the book remains accessible.

It is a book on which I have had to expend great effort. Still, more or less, it came out rather spontaneously. The idea of the images occurred to me as keys which can open up surprising insights. It would be a source of great pleasure to me if the reader's experience is the same.

I have written this book also in order to fulfill an obligation as general secretary (scriba) of the Protestant Church in the Netherlands in this, the second period of my appointment. I hope with this book to contribute to the life of our church, but with the desire also to serve readers from other churches and readers who do not belong to any church. I have not had any specific target group in mind as I wrote. Generally speaking, I intend to address those who consciously busy themselves with questions about God, faith, and church. I have avoid theological language intelligible only to the initiated, insofar as that was feasible. I understand, however, that the style and contents will not be accessible for all readers. Nevertheless, I hope it will be readable for all readers of good will who wish seriously to inform themselves about the Christian tradition, as well as those who stand at a distance from that tradition.

I make no pretensions to scholarship. I have avoided making this a book exclusively one of theology. It is a cross between a theological treatise, a sermon, a meditation, a pastoral conversation, and (sometimes) a philosophical essay. One will find, to be sure, implicit and explicit assertions that I think have theological and philosophical significance. Those who launch antennas for such matters will surely discover them. I am indebted, of course, to many, but I have chosen to keep the number of references to a minimum. Only when I make a direct citation do I name the source.

I thank my brother, Leo, who very patiently gave a thorough reading and in so doing alerted me to many linguistic and grammatical pitfalls. I also thank Guus Labooy, who at an earlier stage raised perceptive questions and also made encouraging observations.

I have reaped many benefits from his work. I thank Sjaak van 't Kruis as my first reader. His encouragement prompted me to continue; his critical comments were more than welcome. And I thank Janet Van Dijk, who went through the final version with a fine-tooth comb.

A closing comment. I have used multiple instances of he, him, and his, where I mean, of course, she and her as well. I hope that my feminine readers have the humor to forgive this one-sidedness.

Arjan Plaisier

Preface

AS ONE MIGHT EXPECT from Dr. Plaisier's position as general secretary of the Protestant Church in the Netherlands, this man is a person "who has been around," and, thus, not surprisingly, his *Deep Calls Unto Deep* is a serious book. He presents the Christian faith to a secular world as a belief structure that addresses mankind's deepest needs. As a prominent leader not only in the Netherlands but in Europe as well, he is ecumenical in his outlook but also serious about the depth and the challenge to belief in the saving gospel as revealed in Holy Scriptures.

This work is not a textbook on systematic theology—though he appears perfectly equipped to author one. Even so, it does present an extensive overview of essences of the heart and soul of the faith. The four parts—Revelation, Faith, the Church, and Verities, or Realities, describe in concrete detail how Plaisier understands the Christian faith and what it means to him. The personal element helps to explain his own description of his work as a "faith book"—a book with some of the characteristics of a devotional element, features which mark him as a caring pastor and teacher. All the while I was engaged with this book, the familiar hymn kept going through my mind, "O love of God, how strong, and true . . . We read thee best in Him who came . . . Our life to live and death to die." The lines in the last verse read, "Eternal love, in thee we rest / Forever safe, forever blest." He views faith as God's abundant love as expressed in the overflowing goodness of his creation, gifts which are entitled to a response from man.

Plaisier's foreword outlines conveniently the structure and purpose of his book. But let me add a few observations. For one thing, having read the book first in its original Dutch, and then in Steve Van der Weele's competent translation, I became impressed with the literary quality of Plaisier's writing. His language is appealing, creative, original, lively; it jumps at the reader as if it were a living vehicle. The writer of the book of Ecclesiastes would surely have made Plaisier's book an exception to his complaint about the surplus of books.

Though he takes his time about getting to the section on The Church, it is central in Plaisier's thinking. He is emphatic about the need for a meaningful relationship with the church as divinely called to proclaim the gospel and to constitute a spirit-filled community. The world's secularism mindset, one too easily content with the "spiritual but not religious" mantra of the day, needs that gospel. I heartily endorse Plaisier's plea to the marginalized; they need to understand that the Church is a gift, and that with its transcendent vision, it can serve the deep human needs as no human institution can. No other organization can duplicate all that gets proclaimed in the eating of the bread and drinking of the wine.

It is for these reasons that I feel privileged to recommend this book. Read, reflect, be edified and grow in your appreciation of the height, depth, and breadth of the gospel.

Sierd J. Woudstra

PART 1

Revelation

1

Introduction

THE LITERARY WORLD SPEAKS of three basic literary forms—namely, the epic, the lyric, and the dramatic. In addition, they will sometimes add a fourth, namely, the didactic. The *epic* is all narrative; it tells a story. It tells a story about fundamental issues; it is comprehensive, a coherent whole. It tells not only what occurred, the events in the story. It also throws light on reality here and now. It is a huge narrative in which people and, sometimes, entire civilizations are identified. The *lyric* does not so much tell a story with beginning and an ending but, rather, interprets a state of mind, a mood, a feeling; it also evokes an emotion, a passion. But lyric also at some point t ells a story, and also reflects reality. However, in doing this, lyric explores the inner life, the heart, the emotions. The *dramatic* moves us into the drama. In drama, action is central. The actions create the tension which are essential to drama. We get players, and it is the interaction between the players which determine the character of the play. Drama does more than present this action. It involves the spectator by what transpires on the stage. One must be able to see himself in the drama. The *didactic*, to conclude, is the form of literature which appeals to our intellect, and does so in more or less scholarly style.

I choose these four literary forms as avenues to clarify something about the revelation of God. We could say nothing about God were he always silent. We would have no experience of God had he not chosen to disclose himself. Without revelation, God is a locked book. I believe that God has indeed revealed himself, and that he has done this especially through language. In the beginning was the Word. That Word has spoken, and it has been interpreted through poets, storytellers, prophets, and teachers. The Word has rung out as a living voice, and then put into written form. For that reason the Holy Scriptures, the Bible, is indispensable for an understanding of God. All the voices and languages spoken return to us in the Bible. The Bible is a book of many genres. It is not accidental that we encounter the four principal forms in the Bible. All four are required if we are to understand something about God. Each of these main forms reveals God to us in its unique way. Not one of them has a monopoly over the other. God reveals himself to us in the epic, the lyric, the dramatic, and doctrine.

Devotional books are ordinarily, by definition, didactic. They set out in more or less an orderly way the contents of the faith. Many manuals follow the sequence of a confession—for example, the Apostle's Creed. Other devotionals follow the form of a catechism—a sort of introduction to the language of the faith, written in prose. Other variants and sequences are possible, and without limit.

It is to no purpose to level objections against the didactic. The Christian faith is not an esoteric, secret body of knowledge which cannot be discussed publicly. Rather, it makes itself available, and for different groups. For that reason, conventional logical sequences are chosen which facilitate pedagogy. Didactic discourse is almost as old as Christendom, and it is not surprising that these resources continue to have potential for anyone to bring about renewal of life. New books on faith will continue to be written—for beginners, for mature folk, and for the newly initiated. Dogmatic, catechetical, and introductions to the Christian faith, more or less of a spiritual quality, of all colors and tastes, constitute an abundance to suit anyone's desires.

But the interpretation of the Christian faith can be helped in significant ways by use of the other literary forms and by an inquiry into what light they can throw on God's revelation. I mean to say that these literary forms, by their unique nature and interpretation of the Christian faith, preceded the didactic form, and the didactic genre is hugely indebted to the other forms that becomes clear from the Bible itself. The Bible narrates a great story. The Bible is, for significant sections, lyrical. And the Bible contains many mini-dramas, though not always cast strictly in pure dramatic form (though the book of Job comes close). The Bible in its entirety can be considered a dramatic work. What do reflections on the three principal forms contribute? What is the great narrative of the Bible? What feelings are evoked, and what responses are called forth? How is the drama between God and man portrayed?

I am convinced that answering these questions can cast light and understanding on God and his revelation and that they give surprising images of the interaction between God and man. I believe also that the existential meaning of belief in God and the living reality of that belief come to the fore when we use these three leading literary forms as keys to discussions about the revelation of God. I will discuss these forms and make some remarks about their relevance. After the "big three" I will close with a modest treatment of the fourth, the didactic.

2

The Epic

The Great Narrative

WE ARE PART OF a great narrative. It is nothing less than the narrative of heaven and earth as it unfolds, from its beginning to the end. It is really a big narrative, and happily so. We cannot live at the level of the small narratives and the minutiae of the day, not even from the sum of our daily narratives. Even if we feel ourselves a one-day butterfly, we need more than the span of a day to spread our wings. Our own narrative unfolds only in the context of a larger narrative. Of course, we live our own lives, modest and unique as they are. It is sometimes a narrative hard to tell—so disordered, so laced with choices, a tale of such fits and starts that one cannot make head or tail of it all—a tale which now leads us in this direction and then again in another. Our narrative is more a contemporary film than a classical novel. But it is just at those times that it is good to remember that our modest narratives are woven into the framework of the larger narrative, an ongoing narrative that runs from the beginning to the end of time.

Who informs us about this Great Narrative? Well, the prophets, and the apostles. The Christian tradition. The Bible itself. And in the wake of all these, we people who are alive today. It is being told and being translated in all languages and tongues. This Great Narrative comes to us in the mosaic of the Bible. We read it in the language of the myth-makers, and from historians, and from evangelists. The word "Epic" intends to define

"The Great Narrative." The Great Story of the Bible is a story of the great happenings in life; it is a story with a high arch, under which are enacted the lives of men and nations. It is a story which has exercised compelling power in the past and still leaves its imprint on the lives of individuals, communities, and cultures.

Is the Great Narrative a Thing of the Past?

According to some spokespersons for postmodernism, the era of the great narrative has permanently vanished. What is left are the small personal stories, incapable of organization, nor are they supposed to be capable of any structure. Life is a fragment. All we can do is make the best of it without racking our brains about what surpasses our understanding. We better busy ourselves with just our small narratives and with the narratives of others that enrich our lives. Great narratives, they say, leave shoes too large for us to fill. Great narratives are, above all, dangerous. They can manipulate and crush; they can frustrate the significance of the innumerable small stories.

No doubt there are great narratives which discourage and oppress, and no doubt when we confront epic narratives, we incur the possibility of that hazard. But that need not be so. The master narratives are concerned with the wherefrom and whereto, with the what and the why. My small narrative revolves around the larger one. Such narratives, therefore, are not the less authentic or unique or adventurous than the larger narrative. Indeed, the great narrative provides a base and a sounding board. Without the larger narrative, the smaller is quickly out of reach. Conversely, the small narrative breathes more freely in the context of the great narrative.

We have many larger narratives. All the great religions have a great story to tell. Sometimes they overlap with each other, sometimes they contradict each other. The great philosophers of the past also told a great story. Sometimes they literally reached out toward the literary character of an epic. The Enlightenment did this. So did the Romantic era. All ideologies do this, whether they are national or cosmopolitan. Darwinism is a great narrative, even as Marxism is. Even some types of nihilism are great narratives, though they may not always succeed in achieving an epic. As long as we remain human, and as long as we continue to address the questions of who we are, where life leads, what our duty is—so long these stories will be told. We cannot escape them. One great narrative differs markedly from another. The great ones sometimes contradict each other. They cannot all be equally true. I believe that one narrative is superior to another. I also believe that the idea that the great narrative is passé is not tenable. That idea reduces the significance of man and causes civilizations to languish.

The Lord of the Rings as Resonance of the Great Narrative

THE CHRISTIAN TRADITION HAS a great story to tell. It gets to be told in many ways and appears in many variations. It gets elucidated in a variety of perspectives; it has been set down with various emphases. Still, the Christian narrative comes with a profile which distinguishes it from other great narratives. It is a narrative with such force that it resonates with many other great narratives.

Now and then such resonance in its turn evokes the Great Narrative. It happened to me when I read *The Lord of the Rings*. What gets told in this great narrative is the story of Middle Earth. Middle Earth is being threatened by Sauron, of the Mordor dynasty, a sinister spirit who wishes to subject everything to his might. He is also searching for a ring which, when it falls into his hands, will give him supreme power. He is particularly eager to rule over mankind and over the city of man and its king. The world, however, is not destined to be under Sauron's power. The world is good, as good as it is in the Shire, a province where the lowly hobbits live. The world is a good creation, founded on a good idea, but also fragile and exceedingly vulnerable. Hostile spirits can invade it and altogether destroy it. Evil spirits are busily at work to drag everything down into darkness.

The book also narrates how Middle Earth is rescued from the evil powers, especially through the resolve of the hobbits Frodo and Sam. It is a breathtaking adventure, one in which the fate of Middle Earth hangs by a thread. Ultimately, however, the powers of darkness are destroyed, and the true king of men manifests himself and, with him, a messianic time. As I have already noted, Tolkien's narrative is an echo of the Bible. "The Old and the New Testament are the great code of Art."[1] As a confessing Roman Catholic, a devotee of the Bible, Tolkien understood this. He had learned from the Bible about a good creation, a contest between good and evil, the redemption of the world through the humble man from Nazareth, and the hope of a new dawn at some blessed time in the future. Tolkien's story is an echo of this narrative.

1. Blake, *Poetry and Prose*, 271.

It is remarkable that Tolkien's chief characters are fully aware that they are part of a great narrative. It is not a narrative which goes over their heads, but one which involves them. They do not create it, but they find themselves in it. Sam the hobbit says, as he finds himself in the same situation. "Why, to think of it, we're in the same tale still! It's going on. Don't the great tales never end?"[2]

The story of which Sam and Frodo are a part is becoming transparent for them as modeled on a basic classical narrative. And, conversely, this classical narrative is time and again actualized. The answer of Prodo at Sam's remark is, "No, the story never ends, but the people who are part of it; they come and, then, when they have finished their role, they go."[3]

The Great Narrative which the Bible relates is equally a story about actors here and now. It is a narrative in which we find ourselves. That is what makes our life so exhilarating. And the narrative does not end; it continues. It has a pattern, and we are allowed to know the direction. But at the same time this story is taking place here and now. The Great Narrative, however, is not all-comprehensive. It is great, but it doesn't transcend its borders. It involves heaven-high dimensions, and it descends into the deep crevices of our lives, yet it is at the same time sober and open. The narrative allows space for the uniquely human fate. It does not compel uniformity or reduce men to stereotypes. It is not so all-powerful that our individual lives are constrained before they begin. Above all, my story adds to the Great Narrative, and that narrative is not indifferent to my own more modest story. At the same time, it is for me and my story also a liberation to be intimately connected to part of the great narrative of God and his world.

The Great Story in a Nutshell

As I have already observed, the Great Narrative of the Christian tradition is one that is always being retold and re-interpreted. I wish now to summarize this story into a nutshell. I have my ear attuned to the Bible, while being guided by a credo as a kind resumé of the Bible.

It begins with the beginning. "In the beginning, God created the heavens and the earth." That is probably the most enigmatic statement to be found anywhere. "In the beginning." What beginning? When was that? And then the words, "God created." God, the eternal one, is from eternity

2. Tolkien, *Two Towers*, 363.

3. Ibid., 924.

to eternity. Then, by something enigmatic (created) we get a heaven and an earth. The eternal God is still an eternal God, but now we also have a heaven and an earth, and God is now also the God of heaven and earth. What will happen to that heaven and earth? What will be its fate?

It is with huge and swift steps that the story of the earth gets told. After six days we have a green planet, surrounded by the sun, and a moon and stars which all bow to this royal being. The earth is fertile, irrigated by water, bathed in light. It swarms with life: birds winging their way in the air, fishes with fins swimming in the water, and men and animals on the vast plains. The story gets told in primal language, punctuated by refrains, and all set in a time frame of seven days. Through the immense universe (to use another kind of language) a tiny stone is speeding. But it is a noble stone, a pearl of great price, conceived in the mind of God, executed by his finger, and declared good by God himself. The heavens and the earth are not God, but they are garments with which he clothes himself, garments with which he has chosen to reveal his everlasting power and deity. So profound is all this, so awesome, so beyond the wisdom of man. Here is the beginning of a story which seemingly is a love story: "And God saw that it was good" (Gen 1:12). On that day he rested from what he had done, in order to converse with the animals in the garden and the human beings in the middle of the garden.

God created. We get this enigmatic word right at the beginning. We are not able to understand it. But without this word we will not understand anything. This is the A of the greater ABC. But B follows A. Creation marks a start, and now the story goes beyond it. There is a heaven and an earth and, therefore, creatures inhabit it. It is not like a painting by a painter; these beings live, and move. And in the middle of this life, from the dashing of the waves to the fish, from the urging of the wind to the birds on the wing, from the motion in the bushes, to the hoofbeats on the earth, the people move. A humble being, vulnerable and fragile, but endowed with the Spirit of God. A child of wonder and not to be kept in a definition anymore—a gulf, broken loose from a glassy sea, rolling and yearning for the eternal shore of the peace of God.

Mankind, earth from earth, lives a life open to heaven. But it is not good for man to be alone. There will be a man and a wife, elders and children, companions and mates. So man will live, among tribes and nations, cities and countries. It is not good for man to be alone; even worse, to be kept alone. He becomes too passive. He must live before the face of God. It is even good that man is eternally recyclable; he is only a bit of organic material who only rises up, thrives for a moment, then gets absorbed into nature and sinks into the waste of oblivion. Man derives from paradise and is intended for paradise.

All well enough. But in the middle of it all comes the downfall. The abyss opens under the human foot, in the heart, between men, a shadow, a murder, a slaughter. Created life experiences the giddiness of freedom. No sooner does mankind look into this abyss but he falls into it. Here begins the actual narrative. The glow of an original paradise remains as the sign of a future hope—a melancholy memory, an ancient tale, a language of freedom. Now begins the long march. Now begins the narrative of estrangement, of surrender, of loss, of illusion, of fool's gold, of blinking towers built on foundations of quicksand. It is a narrative of both courage and pride, successes and failures, greatness and suffering. It is a narrative about the splendor of nature and culture, of iron wrought in the fire, of songs played on the lute, but also of heads which get knocked down, towers that reach too high and then collapse, lamentations and misery, of a broken heart and an emptiness of soul.

But alongside this narrative another story begins. It is the tale of a shepherd who goes after a sheep which has broken out of its pen, or a passionate lover seeking his lost love. It is a tale of risk, one in which not only man, but God himself skirts the gulf and peers into the bottom of the abyss. It is a narrative that begins with Abraham, the patriarch, and that runs through a small line of a particular people, Israel, as a bridge over the abyss. Does the bridge reach the other side? He who reads this tale will wonder greatly about the outcome. Even though we meet great and heroic figures the future will bring, such leaders as Moses, David, and Elijah, the abyss still yawns. Or is the bridge intended to swing over the chasm and to become fastened on the other side? It is Jesus who appears on the other side, the person in whom eternity and time converge and in whom man achieves a firm footing under his feet. It is a unique moment in the Great Narrative; it is the essential point of the story. It is not by accident that of all narratives, this one has become the best known. We hear about it at every Christmas season and at every Eastertide. It is a story that begins with a humble birth, a brief and dramatic life, in love betrayed, but by a love stronger than the betrayal, a love which is proven in death on a cruel cross. The story has engendered thousands of variations—the story of compassion for which one can scarcely find words. It is the story of a love so deep it defies superlatives and comes to us in the simplicity of the gospels of the evangelists.

So, what is the point of it all? Does it come out well? Does the story have "a happy ending"? Now we must come to realize that we sit at the very heart of the story. It is also our story. We live from day to day, positioned between cradle and grave, with our choices, our freedom and constraints. Today's tears cannot be swept away by tomorrow's doings. We are not mere spectators. Even so, we are in the middle of a story which transcends us, which is in advance of us. We do receive hints on the way—the hint that God will be all in all, that the earth will not be annihilated, thrown on the trash heap of a flawed project. The strongest hint is the name in the center of time. The Great Narrative is the powerful narrative of God's love, one which picks up the pieces of our lives and forms us in his image, the image of a God of love. The dark night of hell and death having been overcome, we will awaken to the light of a new morning. God's valuable children will not be consigned to a silent eternity. Heaven and earth, purged by fire and water, will now be made fireproof and waterproof. And we will see God, face to face. That is the ending of one Great Narrative and the beginning of another. That narrative proceeds from the beginning of all beginnings, toward the end of all endings. It is an enormous arch. A high arch. An arch under which human life can flourish in as many variations as man can conceive.

The Great Narrative in the Nursery Tale

The Great Narrative as just narrated (but it can be spelled out in other ways as well) is characterized by enigmatic words like *creation* and *glory, goodness* and *grace, desire* and *deliverance* and *fulfillment*. Other great narratives exist, with different key terms. But with these key terms, *this* Great Narrative drenches reality in *this* light. It is a wondrous light, one which makes human life a scintillating adventure. One could almost say that this narrative speaks the language of a fairy tale. Whoever enters the portals of a nursery tale finds himself in an enchanted world, one which quickens his heart beat. That is even more the case when you enter the action along the lines of the Great Narrative. It is better, perhaps, to say that a fairy tale is more or less a successful reflection of the Great Story. Even more than in the fairy tale, humanity in the world of the Great Narrative moves around where wonders occur—a magic, fascinating world. The Great Narrative informs us that we live in a creation of a powerful magician who has placed us in a high, deep, and mysterious world and who awaits at the ending of a long, long road.

As well in the modern world, which, according to some cultural philosophers, is a world of disenchantment, something of the magical remains. Perhaps it is even easier in this flat, stale world in which we live to nurture a sense of this magic. Whoever opens himself, is receptive, and dares to take the risk will come to see that he has not been born too late.

What Light Gets Shed on Man and His World?

As said earlier, the Great Narrative has entered the world through prophets, seers, apostles, and evangelists. They give us the chronology of God's deeds in his world. The narrative is composed of a variety of small stones. It uses language of myth and of parables, language of history and of imagination. Together they spell out the language of the Great Tradition. We find that narrative in the Bible. We find it in the Christian tradition. Is the narrative true? Can we really believe it? Or has it been overtaken by time, so that we must place it alongside fairy stories with the childhood of the race? Or is it falsified by the facts?

I do not find these appropriate questions. There is not one reason to confine the biblical narrative to the shackles of a fundamentalist approach. The Bible is not a book of scientific data requiring verification. That is not the Bible's purpose. What it is, rather, is a book that strikes reality as it sheds light on the deepest meanings of the universe. It is a Great Narrative, one which answers the questions of what life is all about. The question, thus, is not whether this great story can prevail. What criteria would address such a question? The question is whether the light that shines from the Great Narrative upon man is a light that truly illuminates. The question is how human life appears in the light of the Great Narrative. What horizons does that light open up? Which visions does it reveal? What light does it throw on the heights and depths of human life? How gratifying is that life? How much magnanimity does it radiate? How much space does the story provide for men and communities? What kind of music does it offer to human life, what siren songs are heard, how intense are the SOS sounds concerning human life, how satisfying is it for the human heart? In short, what justice does it do to the mysterious life of mankind?

Ideologies

The Bible gives us a Great Narrative, one which spreads its own light. As I have already said, other stories are in circulation as well. Stories from other religions. Stories from literature, old and new. They will have to be judged on their own merits. The crucial question is this: What light is shown on man and his world in these stories? Where in them do we see the concerns of humanity addressed? How liberating are these stories?

Besides religions, there are ideologies as well. Many of them pose as liberating systems, which they are not. On the contrary. Communism comes to mind, as do socialism, fascism, and capitalism. They also tell a great story, though they seldom have the form of an epic. I am convinced that these stories force reality into a mold and suffocate it. To be sure, they touch on elements of reality and make an appeal to the instincts and yearnings of people. But they obscure things and deeply betray the people.

A narrative that is even less liberating is that of science. That is not supposed to be true of science. Science, strictly speaking, is not a narrative in the sense of an epic. It is a human activity, fascinating, surprising us with unexpected feats, but it does not tell us the from where and the where to. Science often, in fact, overestimates its status with the pretense of constituting the Great Narrative by which the whole of reality will be explained. Anything that lies beyond the pale of this construct is put off to the side and considered irrelevant.

World views of this type have a tendency to employ a form of reasoning which makes their works a form of "nothing else but-ism." The world is nothing, they say, but the end result of a blind big bang. Or, man is nothing but a trained animal. Again, man is concerned solely to enhance his own interest, life being nothing else than having the stronger overcome the weaker. Man is nothing but a combination of love and passion. Man is nothing but the product of social conditioning. Man is nothing more than his brain. And so on.

As already stated, these narratives are put forth with the claim to objective reality. That leads often to unscientific twistings and turnings as they try to lay grip again on everything which escapes these reductionist definitions. The inescapable outcome of these efforts is the belittling of man. In the cause of a rigid scientific protocol, all that rises above the average in man is leveled. And in this account of things, there is very little room for my modest narrative. It is from the start ruled insignificant, or, at best, an example of a universal phenomenon, but not a unique story to which unique names of people are attached. Thus, for the big themes of the real questions of human life and for such individual, unique stories, we can do better by going to the wisdom of the poets, the learned, the philosophers, and, especially, the prophets. Human life then again gets its true proportions, which prompts the heart to beat faster, which gives wings to one's thoughts, and the will room to maneuver. In this realm there is no proving, but there are choices to be made, and science will not decide which theory is true. You have to choose. And every man must make his choice.

3

The Lyric

Introduction

"By the rivers of Babylon we sat down and wept as we remembered Zion. On the willow trees there we hung up our lyres" (Ps 137:1–2). Such was the complaint of the Israelites during their exile in Babylon. But the lyres had not always hung from the willows, nor would they hang on them forever. There is a time when songs are silenced, but there is a time when they are heard once again. Songs of praise and songs of lament, performed for trumpets and stringed instruments, for harp and lyre and flute will return.

The lyric, in the literary vocabulary, is a general term for poems which express personal feelings. Literally, "lyric" describes songs that are sung to the lyre. The lyric has to do with pathos, with emotional life, with feelings, with passion, with the heart. The lyric brings forth moods which seldom, if ever, can be told in prose, but which touch on deep and vital parts in the heart of man. The lyric rouses, unsettles, consoles, gladdens, relaxes. It provides "een levend harten en nieuwe ogen" (quickens the heart and gives a new set of eyes; *Liedboek voor de kerken*, 487:3).

It is misleading, however, to suppose that the lyric spins out only subjective feelings which have no kinship with reality—as if it were a fringe affair, a mere frill which has nothing to say about real life. Lyric can, in a manner of speaking, give reality a voice. To put it even more strongly, there is a reality of the lyric, a reality with an elevated sound, an emotion. The lyric is, therefore, no less valuable than prose or drama. It gives access to dimensions of reality which without lyric would remain hidden.

The Bible and Liturgy

The Bible is not a prosaic book. True, long parts of it have been written in prose, but they are neither boring nor flat. The epic is a thrilling narrative. But besides the role of epic, the Bible contains sections we call lyrics. Lyric breaks through frequently, alternating with the other modes. The designation of lyric is more than a question of form. It is not as if we turn it off and on for variety, as a poem appears in a church bulletin. Even from the perspective of quantity, this does not hold. The book of Psalms consists wholly of songs. A book such as the Song of Solomon is a great poem. Important parts of the prophets' declarations are poetic. Although the New Testament contains few explicitly poetic passages, some do appear. Lyrics appear in the letters of Paul. The gospels, however prosaic, as I am stating here, contains sections that are lyrical.

The lyric is not limited to the Bible. The liturgy of the church draws heavily from the lyric. As the congregation assembles, it will sing. There is a rich treasure of songs which worshippers have taken into their mouths for centuries and which can move people deeply. These are not frivolous or mere marginal embellishments. On the contrary, these songs belong to the very heart of Christian belief as based on the revelation of God.

This is because God's revelation to man meets him in his anxieties, desperation, in his complaints and bitterness, in longing and hope, in ecstasy and joy. This revelation not only meets the condition; it calls it up. All of this—anxieties considered in the light of revelation—leads by itself toward song.

God Reveals Himself in the Lyric

It is significant that God has revealed himself also in the lyric. God openly reveals himself as lyrical, in the mode of poetry and in the key mode of the song. Thus, it is not the case that the lyric has only to do with the human response to God' revelation, which itself is done in prose. God reveals himself to us not only through the great narrative, which tells us about his deeds and about his ways with the world and humanity. God reveals himself also in the lyric. He speaks through the voices of the prophets and the psalmists—and those voices are lyrics. So he uses his voices to make aware and to convict, from the depths, to search and influence.

We can go a step further and assert that God himself is lyrical. That borders on anthropomorphism, a way of man's speaking about God. But there is no other way than using human language when speaking about God. Maybe the one-sided use of prosaic language about God is just that—anthropomorphism. It is a lyrical God that we encounter in the Bible. He is a God who vents wrath, who is jealous, a God who weeps, a God whose very "bowels" impel him to show compassion. He is a God who leaps with joy; in short, an ecstatic God.

Jesus, the Lyrical God

It is in the Son that we can best speak about God as lyrical. Whenever we believe that God appears also as man, and that this man is God's revelation of himself, then it is remarkable that Jesus is a lyrical figure. He has little or nothing in common with a serene wise teacher or a prosaic learned scribe. We also encounter Jesus full of passion and emotion, one who turns the temple tables upside down, who is saddened at the young man who clings tenaciously to his gold, who rejoices when a sinner repents, who in the middle of his daily concerns can cry out, "I love you, Father, Lord of heaven and earth, because you have kept these things from the learned and wise but revealed them unto the simple" (Matt 11:25). Jesus asserts himself powerfully in a lyrical manner when he cries out on the cross, "My God, my God, why have you forsaken me?" (Mark 15:34).

The same evangelist follows this with Jesus' loud cry as he gives up his life's spirit on the cross (Mark 15:37). And what is more lyrical than Jesus' encounter with Mary Magdalene, when Jesus reveals himself through just one word, "Mary." "And the melody / That He gave to me, / Within my heart is ringing" (C. Austin Miles, "In the Garden").

It seems sometimes that in theology and in the church the lyrical God is silenced, suppressed, and the lyrical Jesus is placed in a showcase. The clock is set on prose—one can almost say prosaic. But at this point we ourselves stand silent as lyrical human beings. The lyric has all but moved outside the Christian faith; ultimately, this leads to the loss as well of the lyric as of the Christian belief. The first—the lyric—is shorn of its real object; the second becomes prose, a world view, a set of principles, a set of values, a dogma, and, therefore, a body without a soul. Or, the lyric emigrates from the established churches toward Pentecostal churches where people speak in tongues and give vent to ecstatic bodily movement. That probably appears to our traditional eyes as being without rhyme or reason, as extravagant. That does not mean, however, that established Protestant churches have reasons to feel superior to the Pentecostals.

Lyricism is capable of many voices and forms of expression, of many themes and genres. Of all of these, I intend to choose three—anger, lament, and joy.

Anger

God reveals himself lyrically. It is a lyric which both engages and disturbs us. This is the case especially when it concerns his anger. We get to see a lyric of an angry God, a God whose wrath is kindled against Jacob as a blazing, all-consuming fire (Lam 2:3). This posture may be shocking to us who are accustomed to think in terms of values and ideals and about a God who resembles a benevolent tribal chief. To speak about God as a consuming fire does not appear very tolerant. What crimes have the people committed? What virtues do they lack? Why all this violent reaction against a people who, after all, intended nothing but good?

As obvious as this may all be, it can be a defense of people who are just too civilized and too self-complacent to realize what is going on in the interaction between heaven and earth. If so, they know enough to understand the relationship between heaven and earth. "Divine retribution is to be seen at work, falling from heaven on all the impiety and wickedness of men and women who in their wickedness suppress the truth" (Rom 1:18). An alarming declaration indeed. It is, however, a declaration which we can, mistakenly, neutralize by pointing out that, naturally, it was only a figure of speech intended as the prologue to the theme of reconciliation, which this same Paul writes about later. All is well that ends well, we may wish to say. But in this way, reconciliation is only pacifying a not so very serious anger of God, so that the meaning of reconciliation means very little.

Anger descends from heaven, in the form of dismay at what has happened on the earth. About those alien gods. About perverted social relationships. About bodies corrupted through evil desires. About a culture of keeping up appearances and dark rooms as sites for perverted sexual acts. Anger reveals itself as a response to great cultures that are demolished because they were ripe for just that. Over a community which dances around a golden calf of wealth and gold as if it would never end. On a given day, a furious Moses stands on a platform and hurls two tablets into broken pieces. He has no choice. "I just followed my ways, when suddenly God stepped into my path, seized me and broke my strength" (*Liedboek voor de kerken*, Psalm 102:11).

It is a God of passion that the psalmist encounters here, a God who, through the prophet Jeremiah, appeared in fury in the palace of the kings and just as indignant in the temple of the priests. He is a passionate God who disturbs me, through dreams in the night, through my skin which is peeled off as the detritus of my broken life. These are voices of offended love, actually a form of esteem for the man who could have done otherwise but did differently and who now gets handled not as a feckless urchin, helpless in his plight, but who is taken seriously. Anger is the opposite of indifference. It is the voice of love which cries out and pleads with his lover to come back to him, so that through what appears to be hostility is actually a purification by fire in order that he will be brought back to God and his proper destination.

The pathos erupts in the indignant accusation against Paul when we read, "Saul, Saul, why do you persecute me? Why do you blindly fly into the face of Christ time after time?" This God is not a mere whiner who can be tamed, and certainly not through soothing palaver from peace-loving pastors. "You are the man," the prophet once said to David. That word struck like a brick thrown into a window.

And Jesus revealed this lyric, God's lyric. He observed the city in Galilee and said, "Woe to you, Chorazin, Woe to you, Bethsaida! If the miracles performed in you had taken place in Tyre and Sidon, they would have repented long ago in sackcloth and ashes" (Matt 11:21ff).

It is nonsense to inquire whether the people in Chorazin were so much more evil than people in other cities, or to ask of what specific sin they were perpetrating. It is great folly to think that we receive information in this gospel about two cities in the area of the Sea of Galilee who were gross sinners. The "woe to you" reverberates always—throughout the centuries, everywhere, through cities and towns, through every community. This warning is intended to jangle consciences and rouse people to repentance. For Jesus was here, but we did not recognize him, seek after him, take notice of him, or accept him. We clung to our ordinary habits. We have made a covenant with death and trafficked with the underworld (see Isa 28:18). The passionate "Woe" seeks the pathetic listener—the listener who is ready to stand in the open field and not evade the cleansing effect of the storm by seeking shelter behind a mole hill.

Hidden in the margin of the gospel story, the pathos of the wrath of God achieves an unexpected depth. Those verses record where that wrath touches the Lord's Anointed. The evangelist describes three hours of darkness over the earth, and Jesus in the midst of it. It is as if God had looked too deep into the abyss and fell into it just to be found under his own anger. By no means did the Son distance himself from the people. He stood between men and sought no shelter from the wrath pouring down from heaven. At least, this is what the Christian tradition has whispered with the experienced nerves that become the classical theological tradition. Among all the dying we see the Son. So radically was God willing to fall into the abyss. But Christ did what no mortal could achieve. In the deep darkness he cries out before God and the people, "It is fulfilled." After this, what unfolds is an oasis of stillness in the center of the storm. It is the peace of God which exists from that day to this. It is a peace which still extends as olive oil among people of all languages and nations.

Lament

There is a form of lyric which puts into words a sense of the doom which lies on life and which otherwise would remain unreported. This occurs in the lyric of lament. Many psalms are laments. Indeed, a whole Bible book is devoted to complaints—Lamentations. Lyrics of lament are intended to give a voice to sometimes unnamed miseries, to deprivation, to misfortunes, to loss.

> Israel, upon the heights your beauty lies slain!
> How are the warriors fallen!
> Do not tell it in Gath
> or proclaim it in the streets of Ashkelon,
> in case the Philistine maidens rejoice,
> and the daughters of the uncircumcised exult.
> (2 Sam 1:19–20, 27)

David sang this song when he heard about the death of King Saul and his companion, Jonathan. Lamentation gives a voice to sorrow, dismay, sickness and weakness, exile and imprisonment, injustice and offense. It is a cry from the heart that seeks light in the lamentation.

None of this has anything to do with the pathetic cries of piteous people. To be sure, there are also professional mourners. Jesus sent them out the door when he visited the home of a girl who had died. There are people who pass through the world complaining consistently about being victimized. Their flawed laments can feed on themselves and embitter and injure their inner selves. Complaining people can be struck in a blind alley. None of this receives support in the Bible.

This does not mean promoting the sort of courage always to appear manlike, nor the patience always to endure one's discontents. There is a cover that lies heavily on life and on many a human heart, and the lament helps to lift that cover. What is voiceless, gets a voice. A scream tears the curtain from a speechless sorrow; a song of lament breaks through the impasse of the status quo. That is the purpose of the song of lament and, thus, God reveals himself as the God who awakens the lamenting one back to life.

The lyric of lament is the voice by which grief gets a name. The Bible does not provide an explanation of the grief. The theodicy, an explanation of the grief and the justice of a God who discloses reasons for all misery, is scarcely found in the Bible.

Perhaps we need to insist that it is suspect whenever theodicy becomes the center of theology. At the basis of a theodicy lies the pagan idea that the gods get judged by the success and prosperity they bring. The gods have to prove their worth. In place of an explanation for the misery, words are found to give the grief a name. The psalms are songs which God gives in order to give grief a voice. Even the complaint is directed to God himself. If, on the contrary, man is on the throne, full of bitterness, judging God or denying his existence, then his words will finally come up to a dead end on his lips. Ultimately, the complainer's words will not pass his lips. After the rejection of God, the sorrow intensifies. Now he must search for an authority in this world to blame. In this way, guilt gets tossed back and forth, and the lyric gets altered in a culture of claims.

In the lyrics of the Bible we find God as the place where suffering gets a voice. God reveals himself in the lament addressed to God himself. God's revelation gives voice to the relief through lamentation. That is how man is saved from lethargy and is empowered to move forward. And that is also the experience of the psalmist, that in the complaining there is an answering, an opening. He now believes that where the complaint has an address, his lament will not fade away into a silent universe.

But we must go a step further. God discloses himself not only through poetry of lamentation; He weeps for the terrifying moans of his people, Israel.

> Long have I restrained myself,
> I kept silence and held myself in check;
> Now I groan like a woman in labour
> panting and gasping. (Isa 42:14–15)

But it is in the Son of God that these ideas come to their fullest expression. Jesus spoke the words of lament from his own mouth. He wept over the death of Lazarus and, thus, the tears of God himself became visible. And in the lament of Jesus on the cross—"My God, My God, why have you forsaken me?"—God himself became the lament, a lament directed to God himself. In this plea from Jesus, lonely on the cross, the abandonment, the death, the pain of the innocent, the blood, the sweat and the tears of the children received a voice of flesh and blood of the dying Jesus on the cross. The Bible does not pretend to be a theodicy. The Bible knows well a God who weeps, *de profundis*, from the depths. It is a cry so entirely foreign, so intrusive, that the only fitting answer is the birth of a new heaven and a new earth.

Joy

Anger and complaint weave together through the Bible like threads. But the red thread is unmistakably the song of praise. Sometimes it is hidden, sometimes it yields to another voice, but it is never dumb. The heartbeat of the Bible is the song of joy and ecstasy. The song is contagious. And when it does not catch you and you miss the point—well, that is a sinful state of affairs: "We piped for you and you would not dance" (Matt 11:17).

The music of the flute was not intended for that. It was intended to be heard, and to lead you to the dance. Joy is the red thread which runs through all creation and never breaks off. It sounds like hyperbole, something fanciful, and yet it is the truth. The dominant tone of creation is joy, and it moves forward as a refrain through all history. It keeps cropping up, time after time, and is never subdued:

> Sing a psalm to the Lord, all you his loyal servants;
> give thanks to his holy name.
> In his anger is distress, in his favor there is life
> Tears may linger at nightfall,
> but rejoicing comes in the morning. (Ps 30:4–6)

Anger is given its due, lament finds its breath, but morning brings the song of praise. The lyric of joy and passion continues, and throughout the centuries. It is a joy because of pure existence, because of living with each other, because of the creation, because of the Lord of creation, so that we can live with each other and with creation, the Lord of creation.

The opposite is also the case. It is only through the prism of joy that the veil over creation is lifted up and that the veil over the Lord of creation is removed. The lyric of joy is not an afterthought, as if we make a calculation, find the balance positive, and thus conclude that we can afford a song. Rather, the main direction is always toward the song. Joy is there, a gift from the start, hidden, but not less realistic for all that. It is the expression of creaturely life. It is also the expression of God himself. God discloses himself as the source of joy. God exists as joy. Joy streams from his very being. We hardly know in what way everything is involved in this joy, but the Bible sees how even the trees are clapping their hands. And why do the birds sing, why do the crickets chirp, why do the dolphins leap to the water's surface, why do flowers burst forth, why does the water fall in a waterfall, why does the wind sport itself in a thousand ways, why does water break down into a prism of colors? Is this the lifeless clinging of bells of an empty universe, or are these manifestations of an ecstasy, and is man invited to join in this song? It is an invitation based on the concealed presence of the Lord of creation, who is the source of all joy.

All of this gets a new tone of voice, a new spectrum of emotions centered on the Son of Man. Jesus said, "Can you expect the bridegroom's friends to fast while the bridegroom is with them?" (Mark 2:19). He came to play the flute. He brought the lyric of benediction. "Blessed are the poor in spirit" (Matt 5:3). He came and read one of the most lyrical passages of Isaiah about the spirit of the Lord and said, "Today is this prophecy fulfilled in your ears" (Luke 4:21). Right here, in the presence of the Son of Man, we see lambs leap for joy, doves chatter, the blind are given their sight, the dead are raised. And what is more moving than, "Talita, come." It is almost a pity to have to translate these words, but even the translation is lyrical enough: "Get up, my child." Why do we so often paint such a gloomy picture of Jesus' life? It is as if the fish living in the water of joy lie on dry land.

The garment of joy in which Jesus is wrapped is the garment of the kingdom of God. That kingdom was exemplified in the comparison of the wedding meal, where all who respond to the invitation of joy will attend. All this is more than a story, poetry, pretense. It is reality itself.

It must also be said: Jesus is himself lyrical joy. He represents ecstasy, joy enclosed in flesh and blood. The joy of Jesus is his surrender to God and his kingdom, to the eternal light, to the kingdom of love, a surrender which itself is love. It is a gift of eternal life from one who is love itself. It is a love which has manifested itself in Jesus' life and in his death. The lyric is audible in the likeness of all likenesses, in Jesus himself, the Word which became flesh and which dwelt among us. It is in his flesh that the lyric receives its fullest expression. Chesterton has expressed this in unforgettable language:

> The tremendous figure which fills the Gospels towers in this respect, as in every other, above all the thinkers who ever thought themselves tall. His pathos was natural, almost casual. The Stoics, ancient and modern, were proud of concealing their tears. He never concealed his tears; He showed them plainly on his open face at any daily sight, such as the far sight of his native city. Yet he concealed something. Solemn supermen and imperial diplomatists are proud of restraining their anger. He flung furniture down the front steps of the Temple, and asked men how they expected to escape the damnation of Hell. Yet he restrained something. I say it with reverence; there was in that shattering personality a thread that must be called shyness. There was something that He covered constantly by abrupt silence or impetuous isolation. There was some one thing that was too great for God to show us when He walked upon our earth; and I have sometimes fancied that it was his mirth.[1]

But this joy is not so hidden that it can escape the attention of folk who come into contact with Jesus. It is a joy which perhaps reaches its height in the Eucharist. That is the uppermost lyric. It is a mealtime of joy. "This is my body. This cup is the cup of the new covenant." Men and women come together around the table of the Lord to partake of the bread and the wine. In the bread and wine, the word becomes deed, a surrender, the love of the Lord who arouses us to deep emotion, joy, and sacrifice."

1. Chesterton, *Orthodoxy*, 160.

4

The Dramatic

Introduction

AFTER THE EPIC AND the lyric, the *dramatic* deserves attention as one of the chief divisions of literature. It is simply impossible for us to get a good grasp of God's revelation without the category of the dramatic. In a drama we get performing actors, a plot, a climax, and a resolution. That can be either a happy or a tragic ending. In drama, a performance is launched on a stage. It gets developed and it concludes, and often its effect lingers after the performance is over. In a good drama, the spectators will recognize themselves in the action: *tua res agitur*—this is your business, too, the play says. It is your life and its values that are being made visible before you. The Bible is an enormous dramatic work. It is possible to bring it on to the stage; indeed, many efforts have been made to do just that. What happened especially in the Middle Ages is this, that dramas were performed in the form of so-called mystery plays. In four cycles or sequences the narrative of creation, the sin of disobedience, and God's redemptive program were brought to the stage. This also happened with selected episodes. One thinks, for example, of *Jozef in Dothan* by Joost van den Vondel. And to this very day the Bible still serves as an inspiration for the stage.

The Drama in Mini-Form

In the drama of God's revelation, one does not talk about spectators. The spectator himself is summoned to the stage. Obviously, God is both author and stage manager of the performance and is not to be considered one of the actors. He cannot, in any case, be an actor in the sense that people and groups of people are actors. God embraces the whole venture, and does so continuously. He is both author and stage manager. He creates the very world on which the performance runs its course.

Just as I have done with the epic, the Great Narrative, so I will attempt again to tell that narrative, but this time in the language of the drama. With a bit of imagination, it can be said that this dramatic narrative is told in five acts. The first is the creation of the world, followed by the creation of man and the human race. The Bible records these events in the language of mythology, with Adam and Eve, Cain and Abel as actors, after which other people come into sight.

The first act also provides the stage itself. It has a broad floor, "heaven and earth," upon which humanity finds itself. God is heavily involved, of course, but at a necessary distance. The burning question which arises after the first act is this: Where does the work in its entirety intend to lead? The action is hardly begun before the world is inundated by the deluge that sin causes. And as the flood recedes and the floor of the stage returns, it enacts the absurd and failed Tower of Babel project, which the men in their confusion and distraction are forced to leave behind.

The second act proceeds on a smaller stage. It begins with the calling of Abraham and continues with the calling of Israel as a special people. This is an intense and dramatic scene. Here God is more the dramatist than in the first act. Strong Israelites come forward on to the stage—patriarchs, prophets, priests, kings, men of flesh and blood in their grandeur and misery. Flashes of beauty, flames of justice, and tones of compassion and intimacy come up in this section—words of the prophets who discerned all this above the horizon, prophecies waiting to be fulfilled.

One could describe the play as the wrestling of a people with God and God with his people. In modern terms, we could speak of a love-hate relationship between them. It seems as if they can manage only hostilities toward each other as they constantly break the relationships between them. For the people, this situation is dramatic; it is for God as well. The people become divided into two enclaves—one of ten tribes, the other of two. The first kingdom is ultimately banished, and the second kingdom, also called

Judah, is led into captivity. The resolution of this section appears to be the return of Judah from captivity and the stabilizing of the Judaism that is faithful to the Torah. All this had been announced by the prophets as the apotheosis of Israel's history. On closer examination, however, one could say that crises continue to occur, though with different ingredients. And that leads us to the Third Act.

It is in the third division that the determinative action takes place. In the name of the God of Israel as found in the second part, and with an eye still on the peoples of the first part, something happens that can happen only once: "The Word became Flesh" (John 1:14). God takes upon himself the form of flesh, reality, as we normally understand it. This is an act for which there is no comparison. According to the creeds of the church, God himself now appears on the stage. The drama becomes a "theo-drama."[1] The stage manager can barely be distinguished from the principal character. In a certain sense, they merge into a single identity. This development remains the most amazing and most perilous moment of the entire drama. Some people think this impossible. Some think it is undesirable.

Anyway, that is how the story is told. Now the spotlight falls upon a lesser stage than that of the second part: the life of a man from Nazareth and his followers—fishermen, women, and foreigners. In due time the stage shrinks even more, with a sharp focus around a spot which contains a cross. Here, at this very point, the Word became flesh and blood. It is the central event of the whole work. It is more a humiliation than a deed. Nevertheless, it remains the most significant act. It is the truth around which the whole drama turns. Nothing more dramatic is possible.

All this action, however, takes place concealed, out of sight, unnoticed by the eyes of the great, the rich, and the mighty. It plays itself out in the back street of an outpost of the Roman Empire. "It is fulfilled," the Son cries out on the cross. It is the hour of the redemption of the world. But who knew this? Who was present at the theater on the hill of Golgotha? And of those who stood by, which ones could understand this happening? And who saw the risen Lord? And which of them believed in him?

The Fourth Act narrates how these hidden events came to the light. That happened through the agency of a new actor on the stage, the Spirit of God. It is a continuation of the theo-drama of Act Three. In the days following Pentecost, God poured out his Spirit "on all flesh" (Acts 2:17). God

---

1. See Balthasar, *Theodramatik*, vol. 4.

becomes "God in us." Mankind, Israel, and all people, get to hear the events of Act Three: Jesus Christ breaks through like a liberating power.

The Fourth Act is still in progress. At the beginning, we see the apostles travel throughout the world. Their work enlarges the stage. Beginning from Jerusalem come images of people who had disappeared in the mist of the Tower of Babel episode.

A special role is assigned to the church. The church is the fellowship of all those who have freely surrendered themselves in order to participate in God's drama. They are the men and women and children from all races and languages and tongues who have been given a vision of Jesus Christ and committed themselves to what the witnesses had proclaimed. They look sometimes like loose sand toward each other, but the Holy Spirit, the great actor, binds them together. The Holy Spirit also expanded the horizons of the drama. They seek the farthest reaches of the earth and impel everything toward the future, the final act, the Fifth.

Now we encounter Act Five. We know little about it. It will be the apotheosis. It will be entirely different from what we are able to imagine. But this is certain—it will be good. It will end not as tragedy, but as comedy—comedy in the original sense of that word: a narrative with a happy ending. Or shall we call it a tragi-comedy? Can we, that is, really just forget death, and alienation, and misery? And yet, "All is well that ends well." The drama tilts toward the side of light—toward glory, justice, and peace. Justice and judgment and sentencing having taken place, and all the god-defying banners having been left behind, death and hell and their henchmen will be locked out forever. The children of God will be revealed, and the burden of creation's debris will be discarded.

The Freedom of Mankind

I intend with this figurative use of the drama to make a number of observations and posit a set of questions. These will serve to clarify the relevance of the metaphorical use of the dramatic. In any case, I wish to make clear that we are all participants in a play designed by God. Therefore it is urgent that we play our part. We must first, however, ask whether we can act with spontaneity in such a play. We are neither the authors nor the stage manager. What is more, the control of the outcome is out of our hands. Are we not mere marionettes? What scope, then, do we have for our own performance? What freedom is there for our own insights?

In order to set this question in proper perspective, we need to remember that actors on a stage do not invent the play on the spot. Of course, they are not marionettes, puppets controlled by a hidden stage manager. Actors can perform their roles with great animation and surrender themselves fully to their roles in order to play their part. Their freedom lies not in arbitrary directions. They play their roles. Even so, they are not allowed to take acts into their own hands; even less do they take over the staging of their own play. They are to use their freedom to enflesh their roles, grow deeper into them, and perform their role on the stage in a credible way.

All this has its parallel as we play out the drama of God. Whoever accepts a role in this drama agrees that he is not to find out life for himself and tries to become familiar with the role to which he is called. That is freedom. You are free to choose the role to which you have been called, and free to adopt that role with all the spontaneity and energy you can muster.

> Damit sie sich entscheiden, dazu hab Ich der höchsten
> Freiheit einen Funken in die Kreatur gelegt.
> (To enable them to make choices, I have endowed
> the creatures with the highest freedom.)[2]

To say yes is the highest form of freedom. Freedom harbors the possibility of improvisation. You can tap the full range of your gifts and talents. You are free to pursue excellence in your role. And by doing so, you are not fixed on yourself. The critical point is not that you strut upon the stage but that you participate in the dramatic work. You do not use your freedom in a play that you have written yourself and in which you are the only actor. On careful reflection, it becomes obvious that such would not make for a very good play. Participation in God's drama involves so much more. You enhance yourself to the extent that you are raised above yourself and receive a place in the script of God's drama. You acknowledge your fellow actors, you interact with them and see that they are interacting with you. You discover that you have become part of the performance.

There is a popular idea that being a Christian means that you are bound hand and foot and are not more than a marionette. Living following the rules of a godlike conduct does not appear a tempting prospect. The play of the Christian is ringed around with misunderstandings because Christians sometimes are tempted to engage in spasmodic efforts at legalism. But the heart of the role to which you are called has absolutely nothing to do with

---

2. Hofmannsthal, "Das Salzburger Welttheater," 260.

rules, to say nothing of rules which inhibit spontaneity. Very few rules exist. Of course, there are some, such as the Ten Commandments, but they are primarily rules which were given to set boundaries lest you stray offsides. There are no rules upon which one should develop a fixation. There is a role, a calling, your own contribution, a work that only you and no one else can do. The calling of a Christian gets to be primarily an imitation, an *imitatio*, a copying, with all the gifts and possibilities you possess. It is an imitation of Christ himself. It comes to expression in faith, hope, and love.

The Acts of God

The second issue that arises when justifying the Bible as dramatic is this, How does God fit into the play as actor? The reality of drama, after all, is that it requires action. As was said above, God is not only the eternal silent provider of the stage set, and not only the very basis of everything that exists. He mingles with us, he carries on, and is, in fact, an actor person *sui generis* (one of a kind). He is an actor who ultimately, in his own play, takes upon himself the role of a humble slave, a role which everyone declines.

It is well to remember that God *as actor* is not an ordinary person. He is and remains the mysterious author of a script that had its origins in eternity. He is the stage manager who, with an invisible hand, must contrive to have things turn out fortuitously. Still, it does seem that now and then he reveals himself, incognito, as a mysterious player who instills panic in the evil spirits and prompts lively conjectures by mankind.

That God exhibits himself is not a luxury. It is the answer to a question which rises from the very depths of existence. It is this question: Does God do anything? And, if so, what? As we contemplate the course of the stars and the succession of the seasons, that answer does not fully satisfy. And as we examine the providence which mends and repairs things gone awry, that still does not satisfy us. The final answer is one that points to a hidden history, an act in time. Here and there. Words get spoken, without the verbs, if possible. Bread is distributed, wounds are cared for, hands become pierced—the seeds of a deed which will be manifest forever. That is what he does, which masks an impersonal eternity. That is who he is. Jesus is not the mask of a silent, eternal universe.

God is not a *deus ex machina*, a God who appears on the stage in order to undo the chaos. He comes not as a prominent godlike hero whose role as leading actor is merely to settle a few cases. He is, and remains, God, an eternal mystery, a God who remains far beyond our understanding. But he is very much the God who touched time, manifests himself as a man reduced to broken bones, who has entered history, who identifies himself with us. He comes not only to set things right but in order to liberate history from its futility.

> As we converse, understanding each other well
> There approaches a small Jew, Jesus,
> honnêté or existential.
> He just went to Golgotha.
> A. Marja, *Gewoon*

It is not through principles, not through philosophy or eloquent discourse, most certainly not through a religion or an image of God, but only through an unrepeatable act, that the world becomes cured. It is not through a passive God nor the history between God and man that we receive answers, but through a God who appears on the red way to Jerusalem.

World history is not a serene picture through which we have to look—retrospectively. World history is a stage, a theater, upon which this particular history is happening. The liberation comes not through an idea, but through a deed; it comes not in fine talk but through sacrifice. We do not arrive at eternal truths through abstractions in time. The eternal pierces through the temporal; it becomes a man, a name, a narrative, a choice, a deed, a sacrifice. That is why the device of the stage comprises a basic category if we are to understand anything about life and the relationship between God and men.

Man—Not Spectator, but an Actor

The third issue related to life as drama concerns this question: Is man an actor, or a spectator? Not only does God act. Man acts as well—preferably in his own play, but more often drawn into the plays of others. But an absolute moment will arise when he needs to choose whether to accept a role in God's drama, the moment when he heeds the call to the theatrical community of Christ. Isaiah 6:8-9: "I heard the Lord saying, 'Whom shall I send? Who will go for us?' I said, 'Here am I! Send me.' He replied, 'Go . . .'" That is the mission. Calling and sending are the deliberate beginnings of participation in the theater of God. In the fourth act. The reality of human existence is "Here I am." This reality is not only hidden, but an active choice. There is something finally essential in all this: I cannot do otherwise. In the words of Luther, "Here I stand; I cannot do otherwise." For it is not a matter of now having a world view acknowledging that there is a plurality of world views and that we agree that the highest good is that we respect each other and allow each other freedom. The last is indeed desirable, but faith is something other. Now you will stand on the stage floor where you heard the summons and where you are about to give your answer. The drama of God does not permit of spectators. And if there is some talk about spectators, then it is from concerned onlookers who know they themselves are involved and who identify themselves with the actors.

The role of spectator has become very popular in our day. Stage criticism does not come from the air. Stage criticism by itself is not objectionable, not even when it involves the drama between God and man. For us fellow actors, stage criticism can be wholesome at specified times, when the critic can stand with one foot outside the theater. Critical reflection is a necessity, especially upon one's own role. But it can also get out of hand. It can be criticism from a bystander who has no intention of ever becoming an actor. Such critics can readily resort to a tone of banter, of frivolousness. Such persons act as if they have watched a curiosity. They adopt a tone of superiority. Their tone says, "Listen to me now, the distinguished critic. You need no longer observe the stage; it is enough that you read my review of the play. You need no longer be lured by superficial beauties. I have looked behind the curtain and I know that the whole terrain is fairly flat." He is a critic who subverts criticism.

Criticism is not superfluous. Drama asks for it. But anyone who looks only from the outside cannot know what is occurring on the stage. Criticism then becomes easy, especially whenever the critics resort to bursts of parroting and repeating each other. How interesting can such a critic remain? Indeed, who still reads reviews of a play that has become outdated? An angry critic, after his devastating criticism, might complain, "Is it true—perish the thought!—that such antics continue? Are there still fools who play this game? Of course, fools, colored, and poor people are recruited. But, surely, offer them food and inform them better, and they will stop playing. Or, what, will the play continue even then? Or is it the case that after many theaters have closed shop, others have opened up in unexpected places?"

In any case, the play will continue, generation after generation, with ever newer players, and indeed, despite the critics, after being shunted aside a thousand times, a thousand times will continue.

Is the Drama Not Rigidly Confined to Act Four?

The rendering of God's revelation as drama has made it clear that the dramatic performance continues. The work has advanced to the Fourth Act; the Fifth lies ahead. That may seem a pleasant prospect, but one must not close his eyes to the sense that many prominent folk have, that the play has run its course in the middle of things. To be sure, some people can still be found on the stage, but it is, finally, an empty one. It is going nowhere. It has taken off for somewhere. It obviously belongs to a former age.

"As in Act I, Vladimir stands motionless and bowed."[3] In *Waiting for Godot*, Vladimir and Estragon await the arrival of Godot, but Godot never shows up. Nothing happens, and, finally, the play peters out as well.

The Fourth Act has been around a long time. Too long? It is actually only a nanosecond. The church, the bride of the covenant, has become a prostitute. The deliverance has not arrived, and the terrifying events in the world continue. You might be tempted to doubt that the entire history is a drama divided into five acts. Even the best actors are raising the question about which drama it is in which they are engaged. Many are tempted to merely act out their own play, alone or without others. Though they hope that the play is a comedy, there is a latent fear that it will all end as a tragedy. Who knows whether it is possible that for this generation that would fall out well; after us, the deluge. With any luck, we will live long and well, followed by an easy death suitable for the end of our days.

Indeed, the Fourth Act has already lasted for twenty centuries. Should it have lasted a shorter time? Fearful events happen that no one had anticipated. But is that a reason for canceling the play? What must we think, then, about all those actors who have already inhabited the stage? Think of all they have performed, with vibrancy, with passion, with grace, heavy and solemn as well as with dancing and almost ethereal. Sometimes dabbling in the mud, others performing as light as a summer day. And what must we think about God himself, who has invested himself in the drama? Or about the Holy Spirit, who longs painfully with a creator's urge, and does still long? The play will go on; there is always room for more actors. And every time we look for these new players, here and in other parts of the world. Though we sometimes become weary, God is eternally young, and with every human life the play begins anew.

3. Beckett, *Waiting for Godot*, stage direction for Act 2.

And how about the many times that Christ has been betrayed through his own fellowship? That is the hardest temptation. There is always the tendency for us to use God for our own ends. The church as a fellowship of Christians can mean that, by intent, she herself becomes the chief player. The shadow of the Great Inquisitor looms up once more. Christ then gets assigned a role in the drama that the church will carry out. That is to spoil the play. How often has the Spirit of Christ not tried to break through and the church itself has not offered the strongest resistance? Who would not weep? Have we no reason, as members of the church from all times and places, to confess our sins and cast ourselves on the mercy of God? This damage to the play is not a role the church is called upon to exercise.

And yet, the drama is not ruined. That is because of the patience of God and the unceasing creativity with which the Holy Spirit invests in the drama. Thus, the progress is guaranteed. The amazing drama can endure many mishaps and miseries. It remains God's drama. The Fifth Act will arrive. In spite of everything, an apotheosis will take place.

Tragedy and Comedy

The drama of God will turn out well. But it will have to undergo the excruciating pain of the cross. The tragedy of existence is not to be denied. In a commentary on *King Lear*, by Shakespeare, I said, earlier, there is within the Christian framework room for the tragic. The "My God, my God, why have you forsaken me?" points to the mystery of "God abandoned by God."

This is more than an episode that in the light of the resurrection of Christ must be interpreted as a passing shadow. It is in the very scream emanating from the abandoned Christ that the negativity of existence is pressing together. The tear which runs through all of creation strikes the Son of God and through him reaches God himself.[4]

In the Christian interpretation of such matters, tragedy is located at this point. But death here assumes the character of a sacrifice, from where the fragrance of incense emanates. On the other side is the text of the resurrection.

Our place is not somewhere above the drama. We sit in the very middle of it. Sometimes you don't see it. Sometimes you stay silent. There are calamities before which the only response is silence. Personal tragedies occur which defy explanation. "Wir setzen uns mit Tränen nieder" (We set ourselves down, with tears). So ends *St. Matthew's Passion*, by Bach. The one

4. Plaisier, *Deep Wisdom from Shakespeare's Dramas*, 154.

ATCTION

hope that sustains us is the knowledge that this is not the final act. The end of history has arrived a thousand times, and still it cannot end here: "My soul waits for the Lord, more than watchers for the morning" (Ps 130:6).

5

The Didactic

EPIC, LYRIC, AND THE dramatic are the chief forms of literature. They serve as suitable categories in our attempts to make clear God's revelation to us. But there is a fourth form—the Didactic. This one rests on a different plane from the first three. The first three are pure literary forms. One can hardly say that about the Didactic. Still, it is useful to provide a brief sketch of this form. God is, after all, a didact. The Bible includes didactic passages as well as narrative and lyrical segments. And the didactic has long held a prominent place in the Christian tradition. One might argue that it has occupied too large a place in that tradition, but we cannot ignore it. Creeds and catechisms have played a crucial role in Christianity. Hearers of God's revelation by means of the Great Narrative, the incisive form of the drama, and the poetry of the lyrical know that a moment comes when the reason must work to achieve a declaration about the meaning of what the other forms of revelation have offered.

The didactic element of Christianity teaches us about God and the Christian life. Sometimes, whenever a charismatic mind is involved, the didactic can have an epic, lyric, or dramatic touch. No strict requirements exist about that, and most of the time they do not overlap with each other. Even so, it is important for the didactic to draw from God's revelation in the form in which it is expressed (epic, lyric, dramatic) rather than from other sources. Thus, the didactic can be part of God's revelation and be reveal-ing. It is not accidental that the Bible contains large portions of didactic literature, such as the book of Deuteronomy, the book of Proverbs, and parts of the New Testament letters. These are not out of place in the canon. They sometimes bring a rush of water from the other parts of Scripture into a calmer bed and serve to give the reader a firmer grip on his learning. These passages are no less adventurous. The letters of Paul are forthrightly didactic, but, yet, they set the wheels of his wisdom aflame.

Without the didactic, the Christian faith has no stability. The teaching and the tradition of the teaching are inescapable. We can tell that already from early times. The Apostles Creed, the Lord's Prayer, and the Ten Commandments were regarded as a basic set of resources; these traditional expressions, in turn, were enlarged and extended over time. Since the beginning of Christendom catechumens have been initiated into Christian learning. The word "learning" does not sound pleasant to the ears in modern times, but we cannot exist on allergies. There is surely a golden middle between imposing the truth forcefully and permitting it to lie in the sweepings when it comes to matters of the Christian faith. There is a middle way between merely reciting a lesson and standing speechless with a mouth full of teeth. "Truth" truths have also been preached to us, and why not? God's revelation can be expressed as poetry, existentialism, and narrative. That can obviously overstretch the human capacity for attention. We are for the most part only ordinary, unsophisticated beings. It is therefore profitable for us to listen to what the Christian faith tells us. When that is done right, the doctrines can be presented as high drama and in such a way that it will not be given back as dry hay.

It is nice when, as young people become instructed in the faith, they encounter attractive and creative forms. But things go awry when these same young people have acquired scarcely an idea concerning the Christian religion. We find enough young people in the middle of these attractive forms who now just want to know what, in fact, is the content of Christian faith. The didactic is a noble human enterprise, one which God himself employs. In a culture drenched in information, the didactic gets less attention. We find much more eagerness about such matters in younger cultures. In such continents as Africa and Asia, where Christianity is on the rise, we find a strong desire among the people to learn about God and his relationship to human beings, about the church, and about the Christian life. Someone whose mind is saturated with present culture is unable to experience the fascination of knowledge. And where fascination does exist, it is often directed toward some specialty. An awareness of God as the first subject of knowledge has diminished, as if our understanding is fit for everything except knowledge about God.

Naturally, God is not to be comprehended with the understanding, but we can nevertheless form a notion about him. Whenever knowledge about him is discarded altogether, what happens is that God becomes perceived as a vague shadow. Does he really exist? If so, what can we know about him? Philosophers and theologians were always passionately addressing the question about knowledge concerning God. Is it not a tribute to man's dignity that he should direct his thoughts to God? And does God not dignify us by making himself known? We seek to know him not as an object, nor an ideal, nor anything that can be grasped by the understanding. God always exists beyond human understanding. And yet, we do find words to *express* that he exists beyond our understanding, and we do hear the language in which God makes himself known. It is language which registers impressions and which directs us to him who is more than eye has seen, more than what rises in the heart, and what can never be mirrored by man.

To know this God is not a redundancy. He is the First and the Last. He is the one out of whom, to whom, and through whom all things exist. All things exist insofar as they exist in God. God also stirs our thoughts, and these thoughts find their true fulfillment whenever they are directed to God.

The didactic appears in many forms and contains many topics. Nevertheless, the Christian tradition has generated a paradigm, a statement of basic beliefs. The *credo* of the Apostolic Confession is an expression of these beliefs. Here is the text:

> I believe in God the Father, the Almighty,
> Maker of Heaven and earth,
> And in Jesus Christ, his only Son, our Lord,
> Who was conceived by the Holy Spirit,
> born of the virgin Mary;
> He suffered under Pontius Pilate,
> was crucified, died, and was buried;
> He descended into hell.
> The third day he arose again
> from the dead;
> He ascended into heaven
> and is seated at the right hand of God,
> the Father Almighty;
> from where he shall come to judge the living and the dead.
> I believe in the Holy Spirit,
> I believe in the Holy Catholic Church,

the communion of the saints,
the forgiveness of sins,
the resurrection of the dead,
and in life everlasting.

I Believe

In the following, I don't give a full explication of the credo. I only make a few points at the articles "I believe in God" and the "I believe in God the Father, the Son, and the Holy Spirit." The creed is a confession of faith. Each time it begins with "I believe." The didactic points a way through the mystery of faith. It develops a doctrine, but it is and remains a *faith* doctrine. Detached from faith, no assertion about faith can be proved. A teaching aims more at an initiation than obtaining objective knowledge. Faith is a prior disposition which begins when a man is suffused with the light of God and it is then embedded in a living tradition. Next, a further initiation takes place. Through all of this it becomes obvious that we are not affirming secret knowledge but words that can bear up under the light.

It is in no way a mistake to begin with faith. A man who forever waits for an absolutely certain starting point will never take a plunge into the water. The one who keeps sharpening his knife on theories of cognition before preparing to slice the bread of life will in the long run be no better off and will starve from hunger. Faith is an openness. Not a blind surrender because there is light. There is light from the world, and that calls for surrender and consent. What comes next is further inauguration. But it begins with affirmation, a yielding. Lacking that, the performance will never get underway. Lacking that, the most that will happen is a wearying and endless discussion about the rules of the performance.

I Believe in God

Faith is faith in God. Christian faith points toward God. Everything depends on this belief. To speak about faith without God is to speak about color apart from light. This belief Christianity shares with Judaism and Islam. It also interfaces with more traditional forms of religion. Viewed historically, classical philosophy also points to belief in God.

Belief is not in the first place a system of norms and values. Nor is it before anything else a choice of taste, or lifestyle; it is belief in God. Here the passion of belief resides. Here lies the actual article. God is not an abstract principle, nor a pale retiring being. God is God. He is the unfathomable depth, the eternal source of light, the pinnacle of beauty, the ocean of goodness, the warm heart beating in and behind this world, the truth of all truths. This God is love, a love which brought forth the universe, a love which embraces the universe and brings her home. This is the God who provides the setting which makes life possible, where human beings can thrive. This is the God who hears the cry of the raven, the complaints of an oppressed mankind, and the sinner overtaken by anxiety in the night.

I believe in God. My life is suspended by a silken thread on this belief. Snip the thread, and I fall into a universe without God, without a First and Last, without a from where and a where to, without truth, goodness, and beauty. Then the lights go out, the music ceases, the eternal rustling of the winds of the Holy Spirit die down. The world falls back on itself, a world which doubles itself, triples itself, multiplies itself by the thousands, but it is and remains only this world, a tautology, forever only itself, a dance of death on the brink of a silent abyss, a gesticulation against the background of an empty heaven. If that is the way it is, then so be it, and we need to make the best of it. "I believe in God," however, shows another way. It is a way open to everyone; it begins at the front door of every person. That may not be the preferred highway of these times, but that does not matter. A wagon rut is enough to embark on this road.

I believe in God. It begins not with me, but with God. I am not the center point around which everything revolves. I need to move out of myself so I can fall into the hands of a God who carries us. Faith is the prompting. It is all extrinsic life. We need to have a bearing point outside ourselves—namely, God, who is the object of our constant search.

Father, Son, and Holy Spirit

Faith confesses God. God is defined as Father, Son, and Holy Spirit. God, the eternal light, shatters the prism of revelation into three colors. Thus, we learn that God is to be known as Father, Son, and the Holy Spirit. All the key notes of the Christian tradition will return to the music of this belief and confession. It is the very basis of the Christian faith, the one which distinguishes it from all other religions. Moreover, again, this is not a matter capable of demonstration, but of internal persuasion. I wrote about this earlier, as follows:

> For some the term a three-in-one God is an expression featuring a secretive God whom we make into a species of higher wisdom. We must say first of all that the term three-in-one God is not really the point of it all. The term is merely an effort to put into words that God is single, not multiple, and it will at the same time provide us space to speak about God openly. God reveals himself to us as a trinity: as the Father above us, as the Son with us, and as the Holy Spirit within us.
>
> The English writer G. K. Chesterton had this to say about three-in-oneness: "[It is] as consoling as wine and as open as an English bonfire." That is perhaps a risky comparison, but it is well put. God is not locked up in himself, a distant God. He stands out in the open, and sheds his warmth and love from three angles.[1]

It is important to note that the creed, which speaks about God, actually goes into most details about Jesus Christ. Here history intrudes into the confession of an eternal God. At the very heart of the confession we encounter the life of Jesus. His birth, his death, and his rising from the dead are the three key points cited.

By this arrangement, the creed bypasses a great deal; that, of course, is why it is a creed. The rest we can read in the Bible, where four evangelists provide abundant details. Still, the creed had a purpose in placing a finger on these moments. These are moments, after all, which return to us in the inexhaustible feast days of Christmas, Good Friday, and Easter; thus, these moments are not as inconsequential as they may appear on first glance.

Christmas

Christmas centers on the wonder that eternity entered time. God became man. The Word became flesh; incarnation is the key word here. Only the life that is assumed (the Word was made *flesh*) is saved. God took on human life by coming "in the flesh."

This idea, naturally, is a dangerous one and threatens to throw everything into confusion. God and man, so to speak, have stepped into each other's domains. Have we gone back to pagan times, when the boundaries

---

1. Plaisier, *Protestante kerk in Nederland*, 48.

between the gods and men was only a relative matter? Does Zeus sleep with Diana? No, although in it we sense in paganism a deep yearning for a relationship with the gods. There lives within paganism a hidden dream to share life with the gods. In Christian thought, God remains God and man remains man. Yet, God overrides the boundaries. It is a one-time only event; it is *this* man, Jesus Christ, but at the same time he becomes a representative of *all* men.

In the wake of the Incarnation, we hear new sounds and voices never heard before. Ever since the child of Bethlehem appeared, a wave of godly living has flowed into history. It was godly living that took on the hue of compassion, affection, and generosity. "We saw his glory, . . . full of grace and truth" (John 1:14, 16).

We have seen it. It became palpable, audible. It has become the underpinnings of the lives of people and of a culture. At Christmas time we assemble once again around the feed box in which the child lies, and we sing, "Come, be astonished, people, and see how God loves you" (*Liedboek voor de kerken*, 139:1).

Good Friday

What comes next in the creed, the words "suffered, crucified, died, and was buried; he descended into hell," in combination, impresses us as five fatal drum rolls. How can one derive a Good Friday from this? This always remains the most unsettling and ravishing part of the Christian faith. Here it is surely important to strike the right tone. One can easily construct from these five statements a perfect past, a logical sequence into a theory about a reconciliation between God and man. The disquieting reality is then soon dissipated. It is also possible to devise an interpretation in which all the mystery disappears. Jesus then becomes an idealist or moralist whose death was inherent in his fidelity to his cause.

It is an obvious transition when dealing with the didactic to reflect on the hymnodic culture of the church. The rough-hewn cross on Golgotha is ultimately the one hope in a world gone awry Here is where love bursts into full bloom. Here we position ourselves at the furthest remove from a cold rationalism. Here we encounter "O, we wretched sinners," but also "the wondrous cross on which the prince of glory died." No deeper humanity exists than we find in such hymns. Cross, death, hell are somber words; they exist on the back side of this world. It is tempting to deny them, but they cannot be sponged away. And we need not deny them. There, after all, is the Son. Were he not there, his arrival becomes the occasion for some leisurely speculation, for idealists, a talk show for the cultivated, with nothing for the masses of this world. He is there where the dead reside, the lost, the guilty. And because he is there, death and hell remain on their own. Nowhere can we find anything more luminous than this. And it is for that reason that we call this Friday Good.

Easter

The five tympani-like ominous words are followed by "He arose, and is seated at the right hand of God, the Father Almighty." If the first series of words hurls us into regions of gloom, this series shoots us upward into dizzying heights. It is as if Jesus is transfigured in blazing white light and so disappears from our sight. Here, too, the didactic must be permitted to speak. But to talk about resurrection and ascension is difficult in a context where folk seek to expand their horizons while at the same time their lives are bound by the here and now. Life here and now, limited to a secular existence, is, in fact, too narrow. People are doubled up as a bird that has lost its footing. Death becomes a fitting conclusion to such a one-dimensional world.

The resurrection is the greatest protest against such a life. Jesus has risen from the dead and draws the whole world along with him in his resurrection as by a tow rope. We are intended for greater things. Why are you on this earth? What is your only comfort in life and in death? These are concealed questions that cannot be answered conclusively. "Since all yearnings aspire to eternity, deep desires aspire to a deep eternity" (Nietzsche). Ever since the resurrection, we have been marked as children of the resurrection. It is not accidental that the creed ends with the resurrection of the body and an everlasting life. In the didactics of Christianity, it is explained that the resurrection of the body is the destination of humanity. And it is for that reason that we celebrate Easter.

The Holy Spirit

Although the creed mentions the Holy Spirit only very briefly, we do celebrate the day of Pentecost. Jesus is a holy body, but there is also a holy Spirit. That is because God is high in the heavens, and Jesus has ascended. But the Holy Spirit is near us, and he brings us into the presence of the Father and the Son.

The Spirit is given to us. Faith is not a human performance which makes us "do God"—believe in, and serve God. With the Spirit, it is just the opposite. The Spirit brings God and Jesus into us. The two worlds become one.

It is truly disquieting, such a Spirit. That is to say, in didactics there is a tendency to keep the Spirit at a distance. That gives us the opportunity to manage the doctrine of faith. So, we are the ones on whom God depends. Ultimately, what we know about God is suspended by a thread. In the meantime, we may become bored and impatient about hearing any more about this type of doctrine. Fortunately, the Spirit is there, who gives life and leads us into life.

Perhaps we need not know so much about the Spirit himself as we need to know that he is active. We cannot come much closer than to pray, "Veni Creator Spiritus," but that is already a great deal. Most often we speak about the Holy Spirit with metaphors—fire, breath, warmth, wind. It is not, however, as if the Spirit is an impersonal entity. We use these images in order to clarify the Spirit's relationship to us. It is a power which significantly affects us. It is like a fire that purifies and helps us in the struggle against our inner resistance, including those against God. The Spirit is also a breath which provides light when we get thrown upon ourselves and with our backs to the wall. It is also a source of comfort in the sometimes coldness of our lives and the hostility of society. It is also a wind that blows wherever it wishes, but once it gets us into its grip, it will drive us in a good direction.

PART 2

Faith

1

Introduction

GOD'S REVELATION IS DIRECTED toward human beings and summons them to faith. The Epic, Lyric, and Dramatic sketch out the contours of that revelation, but they also make clear how man responds—how he is addressed and how he becomes incorporated into the faith. Faith is the human response, the acknowledgement of divine revelation. It is the receptivity before God and the surrender to Christ. God has opened himself up to us, and through faith we open ourselves up to God. Without faith, God remains a closed book, and we remain outside the great narrative in relationship to which our own modest narratives acquire their meaning, outside the lyric by which God displays himself, and outside the drama where life and death are enacted. That is a reality, but it eludes us. We stand gazing at it like a donkey at a symphony. We do hear something, but the meaning escapes us. Faith changes all that. Through faith we come under God's sphere of influence and become initiated into his world. We have ears and we begin to hear; we have eyes, and we begin to see.

I do not intend to provide an analysis of faith here. The profile of faith, in fact, can be deduced from passages found in Part 1, Revelation. I much prefer to explore the *gestalt*, or shapes, of faith. Faith takes on various forms. It is well that we make that explicit. Faith incarnated becomes flesh and blood in people's lives. Faith is not first of all a topic of dogmatics, though, to be sure, dogmatics also includes the study of faith. Faith is not some vague notion that amounts to nothing practical or that is impossible to flesh out in life. It is even less a beam of light that lights the sky, but, since it is of short duration, is soon extinguished. That makes faith something unreal, something that finds no lodging in human life. I will not say that you can ever get faith well in hand, or turn it into a project of your own making. Faith is a gift, and is constantly undergoing renewal. This implies that faith is not static, something that you can define once and for all, or something you can put in a drawing. On the other hand, faith is not something beyond one's comprehension. There are believers, people for whom faith becomes a reality. The Bible speaks of Abraham as the father of all believers, and in the letter to the Hebrews it is made clear that in the case of Abraham, Sara, and many others, the faith was manifested in their lives with God. There is continuity in faith, a history of faith, of the role of faith in one's life.

Not much has been written about the shapes that faith takes. That is regrettable. It turns faith into something unreal. Perhaps that neglect comes from fear that to describe the contours of faith assumes the character of directives: this is how you must do it, and other ways are not fruitful. We must, therefore, find a way to avoid that danger. In the next pages I present four profiles of faith. By doing so, I intend to make clear that there is not only one form of faith. True enough, faith points to but one God, but that faith develops in different ways in different people. There is faith in the plural, and there are many faith forms. And each gestalt, or form, will help clarify what faith is.

I distinguish four forms, or shapes, that faith can take: spring, summer, autumn, and winter. This metaphor is only a figure of speech, but it will help us initiate a dialogue about the shapes of belief as we encounter them in the context of our church life and culture. The development of each of these forms should make their usefulness clear. Each season has its beauty, and the same is true when it comes to the respective form of faith. I do not, however, intend, by positing these distinctions, to identify completely a given form of faith with one of the gestalt. We are dealing with types that we never encounter in reality. What is more, these forms in practice blend into each other. Thus, each faith form hopefully partakes of spring, and in all likelihood each faith knows something of the winter in faith. These gestalt blend with each other and sometimes imperceptibly phase into each other. Moreover, one must avoid the trap of making a single form of faith take on the character of a monopoly; each form becomes diseased whenever such an identification is made. Therefore, my description also takes on critical tones. Of course, these critical tones are well-intentioned, as is the positive description.

The book is meant to present "facts on the ground." This is how people believe. I also intend, however, to use my description as a reminder to those whose memory of these matters has become dim. What follows, thus, is an invitation to the type of faith that is described and to remind them of an aspect of faith that may have forgotten. In this chapter I adopt somewhat the role of a pastor reaching out to the reader in the hope that it will help him in his life and faith journey.

2

Spring

The flowers appear in the countryside,
The season of birdsong is come.

—SONG OF SONGS 2:12

THE SPRINGTIME OF FAITH is the time of love. In the book of Revelation we find, in one of the letters, some talk about "the first love" (Rev 2:4). Spring is a mysterious happening. Asleep and growing under the blanket of winter, spring sometimes breaks through in the outdoors in one day. "In een bewogen nacht" (in one eventful night) is how the early morning presents the spring garments: a soft green, impossible to describe. Perhaps you saw it coming: *there is something in the air.* And still spring is a wonder that surprises us, affects us, overwhelms us. The flowers appear on earth. Where do they come from? Out of a shoot from the earth, planted by an elf early one morning? Born out of the high heavens? Or did they originate through the breath of the Spirit? "When you send forth your spirit, they are created, and you give new life to the earth" (Ps 104:30).

Springtime, it is the time when the newly born silly lambs frisk and jump. It is the time when the cows leave their stalls and leap in the meadow. Springtime, that is the time for love. The Song of Songs is a book suited for spring: "Hark! my beloved . . . My beloved spoke, saying to me / Rise up, my darling, / my fair one, come away. For see, the winter is past, the rains are over and gone" (Song 2:8, 10–11).

After the winter, when the mouth was closed shut and life was frozen, spring arrived to drive away the cold, the lovers found their tongues, and life warmed in the spring sunshine. Spring is the time when the icy crust gives way and the winter is freed from its imprisonment, tyranny, and isolation, in order to make way for a "Prague" spring. "In the juvescence of the year came Christ, the tiger" (T. S. Eliot, "Gerontion").

It is striking that the poet sets the coming of Christ in the spring. Jesus and spring time belong together. The winter of God's silence has passed, the flute player plays his unheard melodies and calls the children of the world to begin dancing. That Jesus is called "the tiger" is, incidentally, not accidental. His coming is never all that harmless. The wolves of winter will experience it, and all the ghosts of winter will confront the choice whether to take off their winter garments or to keep them.

Faith and the Springtime of One's Life

One of the forms that faith takes is the spring. Faith awakens, on one day, in the soul, in the body. That faith becomes aroused is a wonder. It could just as well not have happened, and sometimes it does not. Spring, then, never arrives. How does this awakening of faith come about? Does it come from the depths of the narrative of a person's life? Has faith lain dormant as a tiny seed in the depths of the subconscious, waiting for the time when it will germinate? Or is it a breath of heaven that now, in this instant, blows upon a person and makes his faith come alive? We cannot tell. It is a secret not subject to rational inquiry. Anyhow, the wonder of the birth of faith happens. It can happen to a young person. It can happen to a man in the strength of his years. And springtime can occur even in the life of a man who is old and gray. And however it happens, and wherever it manifests itself, faith is no more a product than spring is a product. It is a gift. It appears.

On a certain day, I awaken as a Christian. What has happened during the night? No one knows. Perhaps I had already opened myself to it. Maybe I was simply about to do what I needed to do. Maybe it is the result of intensive introspection or a patient initiation. But even these do not explain everything. In the matter of rebirth or new birth, the rules for it escapes us. Was it the water of baptism that, for a long time, cradled a seed that now comes to life? Infant baptism is such an authentic springtime action, a wetting of a child with an eye on the growth of its faith. We say this is premature, but we surely do not have to keep him ice-bound in winter garments?

It often happens that faith emerges in the springtime of life. This does not make faith an assured possession. Belief in the years of childhood can become passive or all but disappear, only to reappear later in a second spring.

Obviously, things can happen otherwise. Spring can come late, or there has not been a preceding baptism, or the water of baptism gets administered to one as an adult. It is not for nothing that the Bible speaks about a second bath, the bath of regeneration. So many heads, so many stories. Early springs, late springs, but without the stimulus of spring, we cannot make anything happen.

Faith as Spontaneity

Faith is a gift of God, not our own achievement. It is not an artistic masterpiece with a religious overlay. For that reason it is not easy to give an answer to the question why you believe. It is altogether impossible to find reasons for it that have a universal application. Why, actually, do you believe? There are surely enough reasons not to believe? Try, if you wish, to explain all the evil in the world. How do you reconcile it with a God of love? If you can provide an answer to this, then faith becomes a plausible choice.

All this assumes that belief is the result of a rational decision, a weighing of alternatives, a pro and con. It is possible that this is how faith came about in the life of some, but, even then , there was no logical connection between the process of weighing such matters and the belief they settled on. There is something springlike about faith. Flowers bloom only once in the field. Let the flowers, especially, say to us, "All I know is this; I was blind and now I can see" (John 9:25). My eyes may still not be the best, but I see the light of God. I see the world and my life in the light of God. The light has raised me up. Slowly, abruptly, but now I cannot see otherwise.

It is not wrong-headed to ask "why" about faith, but it is not a necessity either. The question can even lie as a disease in the bud of the flowers. It can cause the belief to rust. It can become a worry whether belief is in accordance with facts. It can kill spontaneity. It can become a burden. It can become a problem. "But it is so difficult to believe." Why, then? "Is everything in the Bible true?" And why should I always concern myself with the question whether my eyesight is reliable? Why shouldn't I just look? Perhaps I don't see, but the more I look toward the light, the more I see. Faith is an act of spontaneity, of sight, of hearing, of trust, of surrender. The one who possesses faith may be able to give an account of it, but that is not everybody's gift. And if it is a matter of reasons, it is better to go along with Pascal, who attributes it to the heart rather than the understanding: "The heart has reasons which reason does not know."

Faith as Love

Faith is a gift of spring. Spring is the season of love, the first love. For that reason it can also be said that faith is love, an infatuation of sorts. Light as a feather, the Son of God lit up human kind on the earth for forty days. Soon a voice was heard afterwards in the desert, and good rumors of him were spread throughout the towns and villages. A new life awakened. Faith is a passionate love, a fascination, a dawn ending the night. The Song of Songs is a love song, an erotic song in which a man and a woman are attracted to each other. This love song (and it has every right to that designation) has traditionally been interpreted as a commentary on the relationship between God and his nation Israel, and between Christ and his people. That has unquestionably been a risky venture, and sometimes the horse has lost all sense of direction. Still, abuse does not obliterate good use. Faith is a love, a fascination for God, a love for his Word, a being drawn to God through Christ. For that reason, faith is also a response, a surrender. He who does not understand such language does not know much about the deep soundings of faith.

A fitting symbol of faith can be found in David, the shepherd lad who strummed the lyre, far more than King Saul, with his spear and suit of armor. In spite of the seriousness of faith, in spite of trouble, wavering, and hesitation, in spite of doubts and questions, faith is still an expression of love which lives and beats in the heart. I ask you to recall what I have said earlier about the lyric. Faith is itself a form of lyric. It is love in either case. Perhaps the love comes off as subdued. The Netherlands mentality was for a long time one of sobriety, solemnity. The well-known Calvinistic character traits of the Netherlands people were seriousness, self-control, and diligence. These also shaped the form of people's faith. However, that did not have to exclude love. And if nevertheless that did happen, then the time has come to drop this legacy. I think, though, that it was not Calvinism, but the earlier era of rationalism that played havoc among us and affected the songs of our heart. What came next was a world in which energy was focused solely on success and material gain, which killed the songs completely. Even though this cannot be eradicated, it affects much of life, and the spirit of the age has infected it.

I referred earlier to the Song of Songs as an erotic song between two lovers. It furnishes the language for the love between God and man. One could even say that this love provides a kind of stratum for the love of God. It is difficult for one to love God who has not experienced human love. That is true also if one knows nothing about the beautiful and the good. And it is true as well for one who has no appreciation for nature or for music. Many springs occur in human life, and they are all precious. Faith, properly understood, is no enemy to love and the fragrance of spring, and, in fact, often live closely together. On the other hand, there are enough indications that all the "springs" which we experience in this lower world look for an affirmation from another spring. Every person, whatever his "spring blossoms" may be, or whether he lacks any such, is called upon to reach for a higher level of maturity, to know a deeper love, to embrace the ultimate love. Christ is the ultimate object of human love. No other loves can take his place or fulfill it. The other loves, the earthly loves, play their own valuable roles, but they can also go awry when people turn the objects of their affection into absolutes.

That is not what these objects are for. They are meant to remain transparent and offer a view on what goes beyond earthly love and, thus, be a likeness of more than the world's mysteries (a "gelijkenis van meer dan aards geheimenis," *Liedbook voor de Kerken*, 479:3).

Faith as Radicalism

Faith is not only an experience. Neither is it only an assent of the heart. It is also an act. The spring expression of faith expresses itself in a radical following of Christ. The first pupils of Jesus left their nets behind and followed him. They never looked back. They followed Jesus, with consequences that followed.

Radical choices are still being made, especially by young people. Nets are still abandoned, boundaries are crossed, and hands are being put to the plow. For those on the outside, this is a risky venture, but for those who are thus called, this choice is the only one they are able to make. Sometimes this following looks as if it is the one thing needful. These folk muster the power to bear the rejection of their own secular families during their whole lives and still remain true to their choice for Jesus. They show courage when they stand up for justice in order to accomplish something for the indigent, to care for mother earth, or to protest against a style of living focused solely on material gain. "Power of the youth," says the hymn (*Liedboek voor de Kerken*, 320:2). The older folk have put up with what has happened, but the young still crack the facts for the sake of the truth. This energy of the spring season will always show up again. This may not happen as a comprehensive program to improve the world, in which in just a little time paper work piles up and commissions multiply. Millennium targets hammered out in large assemblies mean well, but one often finds more music in actions performed by small community-based environmentalists. The spring dynamic is a deed, a doing, prompted by love for people on the margins and through a passion for right and truth.

Faith as Pain

Faith always has something springlike. It is always something like a birth. Birth, however, is always accompanied by birth pains. Spring conquers winter. What was frozen fast opens itself up to new growth. This looks like a break. There is a break between believing and non-believing. The transformation from the looks of winter to spring is sometimes a painful break. The soul can be frozen fast in this world, adhering to the ordinary, to the rules, and devoted to tradition. The soul can have lain down in a bed of snow and have died in a life of ease, inertia, and indifference. Spring breaks with this. In the springtime of the world came Christ the tiger. And because this is so, the time of spring is also a time of pain.

> April is the cruelest of months
> Mixing memory and desire.
> (T. S. Eliot, "The Waste Land")

Faith is not only joy; sometimes it is anything but joyful. "Winter kept us warm" (T. S. Eliot). The blanket of snow covers the whole earth. Spring is life, but life is also resurrection from death. And that is an unpleasant experience. Every believer is familiar with this. The awakening of spring's life is an assault on inertia of the soul, the drowsiness which overcame the virgins who awaited the coming of the bridegroom. It is possible to mitigate the pain, but it can never be entirely removed. Belief is a form of folly. It is a disquieting disturbance of ordinary life. Of the tiger it is said, *us he devours*. He devours our old life. Spring flowers erupt from death. "For man to live on this earth is a life long birth pain" (Een mens te zijn op aarde . . . is levenslang geboortepijn; *Liedboek voor de kerken*, 489:1).

In a time when the soul is stuck as if by lime to the comforting benefits of a society which responds to every need, it is not easy to spread the wings of faith. In a community which has permitted seductive cultural practices to come about, it goes against the grain to break with these practices. To do so requires discipline, concentration, prayer, and dedication—all short cuts that don't just happen and are earned only the hard way. Yet it is worth the effort, not because of one or another icy ideal, but in response to the call of the kingdom of God and the siren melodies of the Messiah: "Melting water in the May of your love, O Lord, becomes to me again the rough weather of human society" (trans. Gerrit Achterberg).

Times of Spring in History

There have been times in the history of faith when the gospel was preached, heard, and believed as if it were new. The period that comes first to mind is the era of the first Christian congregations. But the entire period from early Christendom to the time of Emperor Constantine can be seen in this way. We are looking at the time of the writings of the church fathers, a period marked by freshness and exuberance, works which still fascinate us and which, not accidentally, are taking on a new life today. Times of spring occurred time and again in the Middle Ages. Francis of Assisi and his followers are the best known of this movement. With what youthful zest the simple brothers traversed the then-known world in order to remind an old world of the power and beauty of the gospel. The Reformation of the sixteenth century was such a moment, with "the young man Luther" as pioneer (see Erik Erikson, *Young Man Luther: A Study in Psychoanalysis and History*). In the later Protestant tradition we think of the time of the Great Awakening, the movement of Wesley, and, later, the Azusa Street Revival, originating in Los Angeles, and then carried over by the Spirit of Pentecost to Chicago where it so powerfully moved the black folk there. And, in fact, worldwide. But from an entirely different direction, we must recognize the Barchem movement, of the Woodbrokers, also a springtime movement. There have always been occasions of such stirring moments when people were moved to God by the Holy Spirit.

It is not a good practice to look back nostalgically at history. But it is even less advisable to ignore the past or to view it from a great distance, or, worse yet, to view it from a great height. In many ways we live from these spring times. "The Hymn to the Sun" of Francis, Luther's hymns, the hymns of Wesley and his followers—these all belong to the "evergreen" nature of the gospel and move us still in our time. The past is a potential legacy of possibilities and promise. Why can't the Holy Spirit revitalize what has been and set hearts and heads aglow once more? History never repeats itself, but it is the same God who in different circumstances performs wonders and calls into existence what no longer is.

Springtime of Belief

The springtime of faith is the time of first love. Many believers can recall such a time. It is the time when a spark lighted the self, or, even, perhaps, a sudden stroke of light came down from heaven. Sometimes there was a slowly developing quickening of the heart. It is the time when God's presence was a simple reality. It is the time of a breakthrough, conversion, rebirth, awakening, the arrival of joy. Later came the moments when you long for the time when Jesus was a friend and God a vibrant presence. He who knows nothing of such a first love is in danger that his faith misses his soul, life, and heart. Only God knows why one man more than another has these experiences.

Some would have it that these times of first love should be viewed with suspicion. There is a distrust of enthusiasm. That mindset is present in established Protestantism. The church is aging, so the complaint goes, but is that not because such folk have hardly accepted the springtime of faith? Is this because only the sober-minded believers (beware, let them not be too outspoken believers) have citizen rights in the church? Is it because each *gloria* stands under suspicion lest it come at the expense of the *kyrie?* Faith as infatuation is seen as evangelistic fervor. We are well advised to pray God that the inner grayness of our hearts will be blown away through a laughing Spirit. Or must a storm first develop, and the entire tent be blown down? Must a judgment come about first over an apathetic Christianity which has put a damper on enthusiasm and disavowed the first love?

God is love, and we love him in return. Faith is a history of love. Every time anew the deer hops, skips, and leaps over the mountains. Time and again Christ blows the flute and drives the winter away from the soul. He who is no longer moved by the spirit of spring is a stale believer who is in danger of becoming a gloomy, sullen person. He who disavows spring altogether runs the danger of becoming a bitter person. He who does not hope for a new springtime is in danger of quenching the Spirit. But what has been, can return: a second spring, a new time of song once again, because the Spirit is eternally young, and God still has an abundance of spirit.

The Limits of the Spring Gestalt

Faith can exhibit itself in the shape of spring, and some remain in that spirit. They retain a childlikeness forever. They live out of a spontaneous belief and radiate that outward. The flame of their first love remains burning. It is entirely possible that we meet them in the South. It is entirely possible that they have had a Pentecostal streak. Indeed, is tongue speaking also not a form of spring time? It is more stammering than speaking, more music than speech, more ecstasy than disciplined. "Springish" believers are often found in the evangelical spectrum. But there are also other manifestations of spring. They may be folk of a quiet spirit, but they are also authentic, however much they conceal that faith. They can probably sing psalms while not having much to do with evangelical hymns. They may come through as fairly straightforward believers, but even so one can sense the burning heart and living hope.

Springtime believers should not impose their patterns on others whose shape of faith may have a different form. Sometimes spring believers wish to impose their enthusiasm on others. They dictate their experience of God and their first love to others. It soon leads to a selfish trait. They can be irritating toward others who want more depth or like to do their own thinking, and who raise critical questions. There are those who can't tell that much when they are asked about their experience with God. The best of intentions notwithstanding, one with more springlike faith can acquire legalistic attitudes. The spring shape of faith is not the only one. God alone has this prerogative, and he does not permit himself to be understood in just one form. A springlike faith which turns into a whine loses precisely the charm of spring. What begins as gospel can end as law. That makes no one happy. That is not what spring is for either.

3

Summer

Hold everything! Midday sleeps on the fields!
End the singing! Be quiet.
The world is consummated.

—NIETZSCHE, *THUS SPOKE ZARATHUSTRA*,
FOURTH PART, MIDDAY

SUMMER EXHIBITS THE COMPLETE unfolding of what began in the spring. The fascinating appearance of the flowers in the field, the young buds on the branches, the capers of the young lambs can be found again in the restful channels. The earth bathes in the sun. Now and then a shower appears over the land in the wake of a thunderstorm which, in turn, gives way to clearer skies. Everything is developing and is finding its proper forms. A warm sea rinses the body, and soft breezes flow over the beaches. Sailboats glide over the lakes. Children play in the yard. The villages vibrate with life. The sun rises and sets, day after day. Time marches on, but yet stands still. "Now quiet has descended, like summer blossoms in a village" (Achterberg, "Verzoening"). Quiet? Or is this merely a life fulfilled, of strength unfurled, of possibilities realized?

This is an ideal picture for summer. Sometimes it rains all summer. Sometimes the vegetation in the fields gets scorched, and men and animals yearn for rain. "The harvest is past, the summer is ended and we are yet unsaved" (Jer 8:20). Who has not regretted that the summer has passed with a strong sense that it never happened? Still, even these experiences confirm summer as an ideal image, even if it is but a week long.

The Summer Shape of Faith

Can faith also have a summer form? Or is that asking too much? Is faith only a "seeing, only sometimes, for a moment only?" Can we ever go beyond an "I believe, help my unbelief" (Mark 9:24), with the main accent on the unbelief? Is faith not always being tempted, exposed to questions and prone to error, shadowed by doubt and uncertainty? A spring gestalt can be readily envisioned. That is the time of young enthusiasm and the time of the first love. But doesn't this almost automatically turn into a period when that phase passes, where spontaneity is hard to come by, and the handcart of belief rolls along, creaking increasingly out of sight?

This is all too modest. That attitude is also somewhat of a stereotype, as if it is normal, or as if one wishes it were that way. There is certainly a summer shape of faith. The young foaming wine is in bags, ripening. Belief has surely spouted growth. Increasing depth and breadth have occurred. The head has heeded dictation from the heart and has arrived at new insights. The hand and the foot incline more and more toward the laws of God's love. The gifts of the Holy Spirit are seen in the company of the faithful for the benefit of all. The believers, in company with each other, keep growing to maturity. The believer cherishes the overflow of God's goodness.

The letters of Paul especially are full of summer talk about faith. He sees his fellow believers as mature folk: "I thank him for all the enrichment that has come to you in Christ . . . There is indeed no single gift that you lack" (1 Cor 1:5, 7).

Paul is not providing a portrait of a Christian gasping for breath who at any moment can fall out of the boat of belief. To be sure, he knows that the journey is a long one, that temptations will arise, that faith will undergo testing, that the Christian life is something else than a leisurely trip on the ocean of God's mercy. Still, rays of light fall in the life of believers. "Therefore, now that we have been justified through faith, we are at peace with God through our Lord Jesus Christ" (Rom 5:1).

This is the peace which goes beyond the understanding. Here a summer blossoms in the village. It is the peace of God, a peace "which the world cannot give" (John 14:27). It is a peace which, therefore, one can experience even in the heart of a storm.

There are moments of summer in God's revelation. Sometimes they just flash, sometimes they appear to roll over a longer period of time. The people of Israel received a respite from their enemies. Solomon ruled, and Handel gives us an idea in his "The Arrival of the Queen of Sheba" of what abundance and peace are like. Much later in time the people sit in the green grass where Jesus feeds them bread and fish. There are moments when the sun of God's grace descends on the earth. There are incarnational moments when the glory of God appears in the form of a rainbow over the earth. All is well at such times. The cup goes from hand to mouth and back to hand. Nothing more is needed, because it is the Sabbath. The lights shine through the stained glass windows, and the images light up in vivid color.

The Summer Form of the Mind

In the summer form of faith, the head follows and takes up the promptings of the heart. "Faith seeks understanding," so says a classical adage from the world of theology. What holds for theology holds as well in some way for every believer as he undergoes development. Faith opens up a new world, and we are invited to enter it. God stands up for his children, but he upbraids them continuously to promote their maturity. God's world is high, deep, long and broad. Just by ourselves we live in a small world, but God intended for us to feel at home in his world. According to Paul, there is a secret wisdom of God (1 Cor 2:7) which is, however, not so hidden that he does not let us share in it. Like a deep sea diver, the Spirit searches the deep ways of God (2:10), and then comes on to the land to tell us "so that we may know all that God has lavished on us" (2:12). Paul chides the congregation in Corinth for not yet being able to endure solid food, but can take only milk (3:12). They should be done with that. In this he receives support from the writer of Hebrews, who finds it not very rewarding that the readers of his letter have not gone beyond the elementary truths of the Word of God (Heb 5:12). He is ashamed for them that after all these years as Christians, they have not advanced farther on the way of knowledge than when they were children. Spiritual immaturity is no virtue. One has a right to expect that over time they might have developed a sense of discrimination so that they will not be blown away by every wind that blows—also in the church.

The summer character of the faith is the result of a lifelong commitment. That is how we arrive at home in the things of God. We see the beauty of God. We develop a sensitivity for the graces in the kingdom of God. We also develop an ear for the melody of Holy Scripture. We get acquainted with the family of believers. We advance in the art of meditation. We learn to pray and to watch. We become aware of our own heart, but also of the depths of God's love.

The summer characteristics of faith, however, should not be equated with a comprehensive manual of doctrine—to say nothing of the possibility of anyone compiling one. Theology is not for everyone. It is a special gift for which a special education is necessary. The knowledge we are discussing is not so much a theoretical knowledge attained by the scientific method as it is a lively practical knowledge, a knowledge of the head and heart, of life and spirit, acquired during the whole of one's lifetime and a coherent approach to the affairs of everyday life. That does not occur in isolation, in a guild apart, but lies open before every Christian who has lived his whole life committed to the mysteries of the Christian faith.

The Summertime of Character

There is not only a maturing of understanding; there is also a maturing of the Christian *life*. Faith, hope, and love undergo development. The sensitivity grows to judge what is important and what has to be done. Surrender to God and his church grows deeper. A style of life originates in which the patterns of the kingdom of God turns into good habits. One grows up with a heart that allows space for others.

Protestants do not take well to the sense of the concept of saints as found, among others, in the Roman Catholic Church. They very intentionally shrink from that view of things, fearful of worship of saints—fears perhaps exaggerated. But there are also saints without a halo suspended above their heads. They are Christian folk, mature believers who have flourished under the sunshine of God's grace. They come in a variety of sorts and classes—the more ascetic types, the more exuberant ones, the mystical, and the more practical believers, but all have achieved their own individuality. They do not need to be displayed in picture frames from the wall, but they still emit a radiance of one kind or another. None of this occurs automatically. Summer growth occurs only by skillful pruning. Primeval brambles suffocate us, while a garden invites one to a tour of its paths. The life of faith requires boundaries, formation, discipline. These are not never-ending practices which cannot be set on automatic pilot. They are practices that come with a cost, but they produce results.

It is well that there are summer guests among God's children. They radiate goodness. These are not tight-fisted old ladies with a narrow-minded view of the world as they see it through their gimlet eyes. They mirror something of a God whose sun shines on the evil and the good. They help others in their struggles with life. They lend an ear to someone who needs to tell his story, and they can sometimes help another along his way with a single word. "Comforting smell breathed at very entering" (Gerard Manley *Hopkins*, "In the Valley of the Elwy"). The summer guests live by the sunshine of God's grace and radiate that light outward. They dare more and more to surrender themselves to God's love, and they reflect that love toward others. They know of a kingdom that is to come and are able, therefore, to live their lives in hope and also encourage others.

Not everyone is such a summer guest. It would not be correct either to see them as model children of God. There are those who may be enjoying less success, against the headwinds of their lot, who face secret temptations and because of that, are less inclined to evil ways.

Summer, Nature, and Beyond Nature

The summer season is the time when grace comes to development. Grace is not a private domain, a sort of spiritual ghetto. We cannot divide reality into one category called "the natural" and another the "beyond natural." To do so places the "beyond nature" outside of our lives, and it becomes a matter of prestige, a private affair, a sort of hobby for people who have time for such things, or for those more educated in the school of faith. Grace develops in and through natural life; it helps us to experience life in a way that does justice to it. The summer gestalt of belief lets the light of God shine upon life with one another, upon life which binds human beings to each other, upon life of human interactions, upon one's own life, which you have to account for. It is a life which uncovers meaning, including the meaning of what is limited and mortal. It knows about life that floats on the sea of God's glory. It knows about a life of walking on water, since the elements ultimately stand open before God and are bearers of his purpose with the world.

What must be resisted is the temptation to lock life within itself. That caution does not meet with approval in a time when folk would sooner live with their own artistic discoveries than with heavenly light. The prospects for successfully living such a life are not favorable. Entire segments of our existence have been severed from light from above, from grace and goodness, reconciliation and altruism. They have been undercut by regimes which are often artificial and merciless. The light of God trickles through only with difficulty. Naturalism as an idea that this reality is self-contained has the wind in its sails. And in a world of endless palaver, of folk who reduce the world more and more to the horizontal level, one needs to search hard for the pool of water which reflects the heavenly reality.

Even so, there are saintly folk who live in an open world and help others to live in that same world. On a small scale, bread again becomes bread of charity, and water becomes baptismal water. We need fellowship for that. And we have a need for a church. We need churches with towers that point upward and punch a hole in the roof. A church with a liturgy in which earthly and heavenly light greet each other. A community of people who, through their lives with each other, discover that we do not live by bread alone but by every word that proceeds from the mouth of God.

Times of High Achievements in History

Faith has a summer side. It wants to unfold itself; it looks for both height and breadth. Historically speaking, we can see more of this side of summer in one period than in another. I see such a period of greater achievement in the High Middle Ages. It was the time when the yeast of Christian belief entered the dough of the Greek, specifically, Aristotle's system of thought. The universities were creations of the time. With the *Summa* of Thomas and the *Lectura* of Duns Scotus, the high points of theology were reached. And the spirit of the Middle Ages reached its absolute zenith in the awesome cathedrals, Gothic style. Contrary to the idea of the Middle Ages as Dark Ages, often too current in Protestant circles, it is better to see how the sun of Christian belief stood high in the heavens and brought life to a fascinating glow.

I realize that very different interpretations of this time are possible, and that they were in many ways more of a time of promise than a true summer of fulfillment. The Christian spirit, even in this period, had to deal with too much assertion of power and ambition, pomp, and love of ostentation. Everything we see in the forms of history has something provisional about it and is, ultimately, ambivalent. That does not stand in the way of acknowledging high achievements.

There have been many summer characteristics in history, but sometimes they are concentrated in a single form or one person. The music of

Bach is such a summary form: music that reached almost perfect form was found in an inexhaustible body of work. The painting of Rembrandt is another example. In theology as well, summer moments developed. I think, thus, of Karl Barth. After his perceptive springtime work, *Romerbrief*, his *Kirchliche Dogmatik* provided a broad exposition of the confession of God as father, Son, and Holy Spirit. He recounts the long narrative about how the Son has existed from all eternity, dwells on high, at the zenith point, and radiates everything with his light. Evil is the "Nothing" that has to fly. The one question we may wish to ask is whether there can also be too much light, and whether even in theology the mingling of clarity and obscurity could not make it more humanly accessible.

The Prospects for the Guests of Summer

This raises the question once again what the prospects are for the summer of faith. They are not great. The domain of faith in our culture is more a peninsula, scarcely attached to the mainland of life, than it is a continent. The time required for its development undoes us. The inner peace necessary for growth is gone. The coherence among things is lacking. We live from fragment to fragment, episode to episode. So often the barometer stands on "Change" that a real summer is out of the question. The causes are many, but the phenomena are obvious enough to everyone. The summer of faith, thus, will look more like a summer day than as a season.

Fortunately, God is not a follower of trends. For that reason we need not become too pessimistic about our culture nor be persuaded by its philosophies. The Holy Spirit has enough creative power to create summer believers, perhaps today more as character than as knowledge, but the worth of one is no less than the other. Flowers are blooming in the hectic towns, well concealed from the larger public, but no less pleasing to the eye. Ordinary men and women spread a spark of summer life to the blessing of others.

The Summer That Is Yet to Come

The summer shape of faith has its place but encounters the same danger as the spring gestalt. Didn't the theology of Barth already confront that danger? The truly great summer is still to come. Life in the here and now is a provisional arrangement.

The early Christians fought an intense battle against trends held by some endowed, supposedly, with special knowledge, that we already enjoy the blessings of eternity here and now. Contrary to this, Paul emphasized that deliverance is still to come. We live in the hope of salvation. The children of the bridegroom cannot fast as long as the bridegroom is with them, but the day will come when the bridegroom will be taken away, and that will be the time for fasting.

The reasons for fasting are many: a fragmented Christendom, a weakened church, faith communities prone to compromising. Not to mention the groaning of a creation in labor pains, about hunger and thirst, about injustice and corruption, about the calamities and the misfortunes to which the people of this world are exposed. The high days of summer are only signs, neither more nor less than that. They are signs that pass by. A cold blast is sweeping over the world, and God's children are not called upon to retire to sunny terraces. The summer is still to come. God's children themselves must still pass through the portals of death. The world must do so as well. The world, and our lives, do not approach the end toward an eternal light and a new morning without a shock. The Great Summer is yet to come. But it is not yet here, and that is why we look for it with longing eyes.

4

Autumn

Summer ends now; now, barbarous in beauty,
the stooks arise around.

—GERARD MANLEY HOPKINS,
"HURRAHING IN THE HARVEST"

THE SEASONS OF THE year merge into each other. When does summer end and autumn begin? What is late summer, and what is the beginning of autumn? Autumn has two faces. It is on the one hand the time of full maturity, the time of harvest of grapes and other crops. The sower who sowed in tears will reap in joy. The sharp edge of summer heat has passed and the heavens display a different light, a kindly glow over a colorful landscape. The light of summer has brought the fruit to ripeness in autumn. It is the season for discoloration, when green turns into red and brown and yellow.

Autumn is, on the other hand, the time when the leaves fall, the days grow shorter, the time on the calendar when heavy rains lash the fields and the sun no longer gives off the warmth of summer. The voice of autumn is one of melancholy, of loss, of a breaking loose, from cobwebs in the grass and decaying undergrowth in the forest. It is the time of reflection, and the time when life turns inward.

The Shape of Autumn: The Harvest

The autumn chapter of faith displays itself as that of harvest. It fits best with the progress of years. Aging is not only a matter of loss. It is also a consummation of all that has happened during the many years of one's life. The sharp edges have been worn down, and a spirit of charity comes over one's soul. The old man, culturally marginalized, may distribute from the granary of his experience, and there is even a good chance that the young folk will be receptive to it. Older folk, according to the paradigm of Christian faith, are not people who try to suck out what still remains. They are mature believers who can distribute what spring and summer have given them. It is a pitiable culture in which the elderly spasmodically attempt to hold on to summer and go through life like sunburned puppets. What is more, since the summer sky is no longer to be found in the heavens, such piteous folk become confused when as they live together in the same society as believers, they have little to offer but their wealth.

The Autumn Shape of Belief: Loss

I wish now to point out the autumn of faith as a time of loss. Summer foliage represents a fulfillment of faith; autumn brings us many stains on the cabbage. The certainties of an earlier time have disappeared. Hope must be based on for the most part without the answers of yesterday. The Christian life has lost its moorings which, stamped with the markings of Christian faith, offered culture. Life has proceeded further. The protecting circle of household, family, and trusted faith fellowship has fallen away.

Summer is gone. I believe that this reality is to be taken seriously in the Netherlands. We have not that much insulation about us. The time for a complete introduction to the faith seems past, though it would be fortunate if someone plucky enough to go against the grain what undertake such an effort. In a Christian life carefully defined, until "valued, small talk, and face to face" fittingly describes the lost. Anyone who wants still to call us back to life makes an antique object of the faith. A rich inner life is rare, and a well-ordered life is more of a suggestion than a reality. All of this can be judged differently. It can also be seen as painful loss. It can also be seen as liberation. The ballast has been thrown overboard and the ship sails gleefully on its way. Well, then, much of that is now gone.

Loss can also have relevance for "Christian Netherlands." Belief played out in a robust church life. The church was close by. The trio of church-school-family was harmonious. Church and social life overlapped a great deal.

Meanwhile, it is very different now. Church life has fallen off, the church has a bad reputation, congregations diminish, church buildings are abandoned, and the number of visitors to church services has hit bottom. The young grow up in a climate in which the ABC's of the Christian faith are unintelligible or ignored. This, too, is loss. Loss that sometimes elicits melancholy. Loss that sometimes makes one weep. Others assert that things are as they are, and we need not turn back with nostalgia, as if things were better then.

Loss as Beginning of the End

Loss can lead up to the beginning of the end. That occurs especially when the Christian faith loses its identity. It occurs when God becomes the unknowable one about whom we can say nothing, and when Jesus is a name that appears on the census register. It occurs when fashionable theologians keep company with postmodern ventures. Unfortunately, nowadays liberal theologians keep company with modern or postmodern thinkers, who, formerly, with the theologians such as Roessingh and Heering, were a lot more substantive. To be sure, this is not only a matter of liberal theology, but we see it everywhere in theology, openly or concealed.

The harvest time of faith can be a time of death, a faith without a future. It is a faith that has lost its warmth and conviction and about which, understandably, no one gets excited. There is no eros left to arouse. "This is the way the world ends, not with a bang but a whimper" (T. S. Eliot, "The Hollow Men"). Faith can take many shapes, but it can also evaporate and disappear. The result of all the remedies attempting to keep up with the times can be the loss of what genuine faith is all about. The praiseworthy efforts to give one's contemporaries entrance to the Christian faith and remove all obstacles may, in retrospect, have been the gangplank over which we ourselves left the ship of the church.

Loss as Gain

There are other forms of autumn loss, such as the form "I will accept loss." That is to say, there is more to acknowledge than loss. This is said in the context of such a statement as "That is why I am still a Christian." Faith has become more fragmented than in the past. But it has not lost color or shape. Perhaps there is just more color and variety, more colors than one could have anticipated from the palette of earlier times. You can divest yourself of a great deal and thereby achieve a purer sense of God. Much of what has been part of you has gone, but Christ still dwells in your soul. Your fellowship with the church has become marginal, but that has disclosed the relevance of the two or three together in the name of Christ. The shape of what has been lost was perhaps more a matter of culture than of faith. And many of the certainties of yesterday were less certainties which were based on faith in God's deeds than in your world picture which failed to bridge that gap. The variegated bounty of summer produced so many leaves that the trunk was no longer visible. The scientific critics have stripped so many leaves and branches that we feared for the trees. The tree, however, has remained sturdy and erect, somewhat diminished, but not essentially less than before.

All this is not to deny that to take leave of a Christian culture can be painful. The Christian culture offered much of what is good. We could put up a good front, with life predictable and almost lifelike. Living in a post-Christian era as a believer confronts you with a much denuded landscape. You can easily lose your way, and sometimes you follow a lonely path. You think of an earlier time when you "marched in the ranks of the great to God's house" (Ps 42:5). Now you hasten by yourself, early in the morning, to church. You feel sometimes like a member of an abandoned crowd. The footmarks of church and faith have all but vanished. In the market place of life, the church no longer has a stall. That does something to faith. That does something to *your* faith.

And, still, faith has not vanished altogether. The purifying fires can be wholesome. We are talking about "A beneficial crisis" (Offring) in which the flame of faith is being rekindled. "God is with us evenings and mornings, and surely every new day" (*Liedboek voor de kerken*, 398:7). It is time for concentration. The times have made it necessary. It is time to reflect on what has been from the beginning, is now, and always shall be until the end of time. It is the time to hear, "Jesus Christ is the same yesterday, today, and forever" (Heb 13:8). Much church life has been brushed aside. The autumn storm descends on it. We know good will come of it. The little shoots get blown away. Though you cannot see it, the hail is striking your own heirs— a stroke of God's judgment? The image of the man leading the charge, the hero of past events, has turned pale; he had stood as well as a symbol for the church or group. This all now lies in the dust. The hymn is fitting: "Brother and sisters long lost, I find once again the one to whom I belong" (ibid., 453:3). Thus, loss becomes gain.

And, thus, there is a faith shape from which the truth of "from cover to cover" has been exposed. That coincides with the flaming heart of the Bible. There is a faith shape which is no longer delivered in a three-part package, but more as an everyday working formula. That may sometimes be difficult to accept, but it also provides an opportunity to learn what it means to be a Christian in our daily life. So we live, so we walk the path, sometimes with animation, sometimes more soberly, but still in faith and in a positive spirit.

Harvest Time and the Twenty-First Century

I believe that we in the Western world, namely, Western Europe, are positioned at a critical moment in the autumn of belief. The thesis defends itself; we have been there for many centuries, surely when we look at the theology of the last two centuries. Yes, autumn of the church and Christendom in the Occident. True, the autumn time has yielded much that is good. The riot of autumnal colors mirrors the many-colored opulence of theological literature. Much of it is another illusion gone, to be found only in dusty attics, but much of it is still accessible, surprising, and timely. Autumn is the time when "a thousand leaves turn color." It is autumn in church and Christendom in the Western world, both with its glories and its follies, enriched by many experiments, and at the same time gray with the mold of abandoned belief.

Many autumns have passed, though no two are alike. Well known is the book *The Waning of the Middle Ages* by the historian J. Huizinga. The late Middle Ages are indeed a sort of autumnal season, an outgrowth of what the high Middle Ages had accomplished until then, but also an "overgrowth": cathedrals which reached too high into the sky, super subtle philosophical distinctions carried too far, an eye for the particular at the expense of the universal, and the period when "nature and grace" merged with each other. The fourteenth and fifteenth century are "the end of the Middle Ages, the medieval civilization, the last time of their last tidal wave as a tree with over-ripe fruit, with everything given full scope and highly developed" (Huizinga, *Waning of the Middle Ages*, xix). At the same time it is a period of "life's passion" (ibid., 1–24), not of world weariness. And it is also the matrix for the Renaissance and Reformation. Here especially the many-hued autumn erupted in vivid colors.

Another autumn season is that of the middle of the eighteenth century. At first sight a calm century, with thoughtful theologians and calm faith. A closer look, however, reveals it to be a rather sterile time, which produced hardly any high points and has, therefore, left few footprints behind. Here autumn hit rock bottom.

What is our autumn situation now? And where is it going? We cannot say much about that. Will the youthful Christian movement from the South become contagious? Will small "spring" groups arise? We cannot know that. Only God does. It is an acquisition in itself for one in his own time to discern, with some courage, just where his time is positioned in the flow of the centuries. We should not be too quick to call our state a winter gestalt, to insist that everything is collapsing, and that the church will disappear. We need even less to report that it is good that the church should decline, so that it will rightly decrease in importance.

On the contrary, I must report my suspicions of the numerous and varied spontaneous movements which are offered as solutions and which present themselves as harbingers of spring. Certainly, let freedom ring, and let there be plucky experimentation. Old forms will disappear and new ones will arise. But I would rather have that done with a minimum of trumpet rolls, as if the new are the greatest wonder of church history of the twenty-first century, posing as a pioneer or prophet out of America addressing us from a mountain top. Until further notice, I do not believe in such efforts. We are living in this time, and we cannot just jump out of it. We are Christians in the Occident. We do not boast about that. We do not look down on the youthful effervescence of African Christians. We remind ourselves that we had our turn in that array, and do well to remember the words of Gerrit Achterberg: "With wide open mouths and jaws, we sing out like crazy fanatics" (Achterberg, "Horeb"). In the meantime, we live here and now, in a sort of matter of fact, unremarkable way, in the faith that God has charity enough to let us live and to let something of ourselves remain. We do that as called believers, without being drawn back to unproductive lives. We need not perform in the world as bewildered folk. We are also invited to say, "I believe," and to do so without embarrassment or timidity. At the same time we know that we exist as people "out of breath," and that we are not one of the high and mighty. So it is. And we are called to love God above all, and our neighbors as ourselves.

The Borders of the Autumn Gestalt

We are unable to choose for ourselves when we will live, and even less under what circumstances we will live during our journey of faith. If we still live today as autumn believers, it is as it is. At the same time, this form of faith can turn upon itself and lock itself in. We can as autumn believers be blown about like dust and let ourselves heedlessly watch our hair turn gray. The knees become rigid. They will no longer bend—neither before God nor in modesty. And no longer will they let us dance out of sheer joy. Then we can no longer express ourselves physically, and so we take pleasure from our inner life. But we soon lose our grip on our inner life. Then our faith begins to become hazy, and out of the mist we turn in the long run to God himself. A mood of *deja vu* sweeps over us, or, worse yet, of surfeit. We are above all tolerant, and we are generous in our respect. *Tout comprendre, c'est tout pardonner* (To know everything is to forgive everything). We live as "a sadder man, a wiser man," which none other than Samuel Coleridge then follows with "He rose the morrow morn" (Samuel Taylor Coleridge, "Rime of the Ancient Mariner"). We no longer walk briskly, and we do not take chances in order to live outside of ourselves. Only out of sheer deference is an outsider able to suspect that we are a Christian. Without a spark of the absurdity of spring or without the summer sun, the autumn gestalt turns brown around the edges. Here it appears that we believe only in our own resources, no longer facing what Moses faced, in obedience, at the burning bush, no longer moved by the thunder of God's word, no longer touched by the sigh of a cool wind in which we hear the living voice of God. And we are no longer happy as children of God.

It remains to be seen whether we remain believers. The summons to return to our first love should continue to perturb us. Also, as self-contained believers we shall never be able to know without the Lord, who walks with us on the way, who lives under our roof, and who leaves us with burning hearts.

5

Winter

Through the dark cold and the empty desolation,
The wave cry, the wind cry

—T. S. ELIOT, *FOUR QUARTETS*, "EAST COKER"

WINTER IS THE TIME when the fields lie idle, the trees appear as bleached skeletons against the afternoon sky, the rains fall upon hard ground without the promise of fruit or fertility. The last of the harvest has been brought in. It is warm in the barn, cold outdoors, chilly and empty. Later on, as the winter settles in, it becomes freezing cold, as the sun shining on the ice causes a fierce glare, a fiery sun which is more capable of blinding the eye than the summer sun at its zenith. The snow falls silently during the night, and in the morning we hold our breath. Where is the fairy who turned all the trees into brides? How did it happen that the old and abandoned fields have become so virginally white? Who has quieted the earth as if it awaits the bridegroom?

Winter Forms as the End of Faith

There is a winter of death. That is no longer a *form* of faith, but an *end* of faith. Faith can perish. It may just have moldered. It may be that a catastrophic experience has totally undermined one's faith. Or, on a closer look, it may be that the faith existed in the realm of fantasy. Sometimes atheism comes stalking in triumphantly. A child may have faith, but the mature person liberates himself from this illusion and travels by his own compass.

Faith can disintegrate, slowly and imperceptibly, without any sense of loss. Life smiles from all sides, and you can go on without faith, perhaps even better without it than with it. One can, nevertheless, look back feeling a twinge of regret, a sense of loss and loneliness. The coffin of faith can be laid to rest in the grave of the past. There is no sense of relief; there is only a quiet mourning. No one is aware of this, but in the forgotten blink of an eye you regret the former times when you could still believe. Who will bring me back to the land of my youth? Where is the path to childhood? What's past is past; faith once was, it is still something we long for, but it cannot be retrieved.

Nietzsche's take on faith as a winter guest was a radical one. Speaking for the foolish ones in the marketplace of ideas, he proclaimed that God is dead, and, with a shudder of fear, he said,

> What have we done to detach the earth from the sun? Where are we going now? Haven't we ended up in a free fall? backward, forward, sideways in all directions. Is there still a below and above? Are we not blind folk going through an endless night? Isn't the empty space hitting us, Hasn't it got colder and colder? Isn't each night followed by always more nights? Isn't it time to light the lanterns in midday?[1]

Who will pronounce judgment over people such as these? Who will so much as dare to challenge this verdict? There is One who will do that. One who knows our weaknesses and the hurts of the soul, the possibilities and the impossibilities of our understanding. One who knows this winter guest better than they know themselves.

The Absence of God

Winter is not only the end of faith. It is also a shape of faith. Every believer can recapture it, and sooner or later most of them actually fall into it. It is the winter of the absence of God. The faith lacks experience. The prayers and the rituals furnish no satisfaction and do not touch the soul. God is hidden. He is silent. Life inches forward. You are not thinking of saying farewell to church and faith. You still look like a Christian, and yet there is

---

1. Nietzsche, *Fröhliche Wissenschaft*, part 3, 125.

an absence of depth, of love, of the presence of God, of spring breezes and summer warmth. Once there was a time of enlightenment, the moment when the glory of the Lord revealed itself to you, but that was long ago, and since then it has become quiet. The heavens are deaf, the walls of the heart are no longer made to shake from excitement. What does remain is a deep longing for what has been and what, one hopes, can come again. You have to make do with the belief that God, despite this absence from your life, can still be trusted and that your life is still secure in God.

Winter, the absence of the experience of God. Perhaps it was only in a time of crisis, of mourning, that you longed for comfort, for the quiet voice in your heart. But the heart remained silent, and the comfort was not forthcoming. It was winter in the soul. Others quoted words of Scripture to you, but you turned them down, they did not grip you, you had the feeling that people did not understand you, and not God either. "They pronounce God and make smoke" (Achterberg, "Job"). Preaching that made you sick.

Many have come through this winter by taking the next step. Or by going along with the church, stubbornly persisting. Although that was not a response to the absence of God, still it was of some help. On this path, there was still some warmth, some vibrancy, and sometimes in the middle of the winter a summer day would appear, in which you could bask. A hymn could break through in an unexpected moment, a bird pecks against the window, you opened the window and smelled the spring.

Does the Winter Belong Here?

Is there any escape to be had from the winter of the soul? Or is that part of faith? I am inclined to answer Yes to the last question. It speaks at least of a lack of mercy when the winter guests feel locked out. The tones of the Hallelujah can become a form of terror, intensifying the winter of the soul.

The winter shape of faith concerns the experience of a God who is in hiding. This hiddenness is the reverse of the experience of his presence, and of life with God. God approaches, but for some inexplicable reason, he can also withdraw himself at least from the experience of human beings. Does that happen because men must learn not to trust their own experiences of God, but, rather, in God himself? Must he learn to believe, also without seeing him, feeling him, tasting him? I cannot answer that. There is, and remains, something enigmatic about a God who is so near who can yet be so far away. Strange, that the very God who has become flesh and who has poured his spirit "on all flesh" can be felt as someone so near who can seem light years away? Or is this the heart of it, that we cannot miss a high and distant God, but miss a God who comes near to us?

Winter time is apparently an inevitable aspect of living by faith. God is not someone we can just summon at will. Since even inspiration is not like that, and inspired writers are familiar with writer's block, what makes us think that God might be different? If there should always be a bridge we could walk across whenever we want to walk into God's world, then God's world becomes an enlargement of our own world. God is different. He is often more object of longing than of its satisfaction. "I have tasted it, and now I hunger and thirst," Augustine wrote, and this well-seasoned Christian understood this experience.[2] A God whom only I ever experience is a God for my convenience, and it is possible that his greatness will reveal itself through silence.

There are moments when I feel more kinship with a bare winter landscape than by the multicolored joyful flowers of Christians who always only desire, know, and feel. There are moments when I prefer the icy frost flowers on the frozen window above weak, faded tulips of the mind and red roses of the heart as well. Things can be too beautiful. One can also be too pious, too joyful, too liberated, too holy, too heavenly oriented. I can believe that there are people who sneak away from overly gilded halls or buildings to wait for God in a cold winter hut. To be silent and to listen. To leave and listen. "Through the dark cold and the empty desolation, / The wave cry, the wind cry" (T. S. Eliot, *Four Quartets*, "East Coker"). They leave not because God has become too much for them, but because God has become buried under the streamers of Christian sounds of revelry. Perhaps God is more at home somewhere in a hut in a field outdoors than at a feast of self-sufficient Christian revelers. The earth there is cold, but the atmosphere is bright. The paintings are off the wall, the screens are closed, because God and the soul are together by themselves.

The white walls from the church painter Pieter Jansz. Saenredam (1597–1665) come to mind. Empty rooms, high arches, no altar, no images, not even chairs or benches, just a single pulpit, and still the aura of devotion is palpable. Here one removes one's shoes, covers the face, and kneels down in prayer. Here there is silence, since God speaks. Here the winter, like an iconoclast, has blown through the halls, but he who has turned his ear to

---

2. Augustine, *Confessions*, book 10, XXVII, 38.

hear picks up a wonderful message in the empty space, and he who opens his heart can sense the peace of God which passes all understanding.

The Dark Night of the Soul

An acute form of the winter *gestalt*, an elaboration of what has been described above, is that of the mystic tradition. This involves "the dark night of the soul." An apt comparison can be made with the winter of the soul. As St. John of the Cross puts it, "This night (the one in which God encounters man) God carries out in man's soul two kinds of darkness or purification, reconciling the two impulses in man, namely, the impulse to meditate [outward] and that of the spirit [the inner life]."[3]

In the first night the organs of sense become purified and spiritualized, and in the second, the soul aspires to God himself. This journey leads through the night to the fire of divine love, to God, who is love itself. This goes on—so it is said—all through the night. It is the night of aridity of soul, the absence or the consolation of God. The night of the soul is like a winter. That can make for a long and lonesome winter one has to go through. A spiritual companion is needed to avoid perishing in the winter.

It is through temptation and the struggle against it that the pilgrim arrives at the temple of God's love. That is the final goal of the night of the soul. Finally, there is a sight of God, the winter sun which shines from the depths like a sheet of ice. Then light and soul touch each other to such an extent that the soul itself burns with love, so much so that one sometimes has the sense as if sun and soul melt into each other. There is, however, in the Christian mystical tradition, no mention of this fusion. God is God, and we are people; also we are the beneficiaries of the life that comes from God himself. In mysticism relating to the bride, there is talk about union, but bride and bridegroom remain separate entities.

The journey through the night is, thus, not an end in itself. As John of the Cross describes it, it has to do with purification. Sense perception is the bearer of the experience of God. It is a bridge to God. A moment comes when the bridge is drawn up to prevent man from depending on it instead of on God himself. The same holds true for the perception and experience of the soul. The soul can also attach itself to the bridge. For that reason that experience, too, must be dropped. Then comes the experience of God

3. John of the Cross, *Dark Night*, 83.

in place of God himself. One then releases the experience. Thus, the soul becomes ripe before God.

These mystical experiences are sometimes labeled as elitist. I would prefer to call them strict. As these folk have it, the soul must detach itself from itself in order to focus solely on God. The soul turns wintry so as no longer to adorn itself with its own leaves but instead opens itself fully to God. As the poet puts it,

> In order to possess what you do not possess
> You must go by way of dispossession.
> In order to arrive at what you are not
> You must go through the way in which you are not.
> (T. S. Eliot, *Four Quartets*, "Dry Salvages")

Only as we come before him with empty hands—so they put it—can we receive the gift of God. Only as we leave everything behind will we arrive in the land that God has promised. But this is an astonishing truth they would have us believe—that what concerns me goes contrary to the very heart of the Christian faith, where the cross occupies a central place. We die with Christ, dead to everything—as they put it—in which we can take pride. He who undergoes the water of baptism, in their view, must surrender even all spiritual baggage in order to rise up newborn from the water.

Surely danger attends the way of the mystics. It is a form of stripping the soul, making it appear naked before God. Is that necessary? Is that desirable? Does not this contradict the event in which God has come in the flesh in order that the Spirit may plead for us (Rom 8:20)? Do we not have here a dangerous flight of bees aspiring to "purer" honey (Nijhoff, "Song of the Foolish Bees")? They leave their hives, go on a rampage, and disappear out of sight. The story gives us the ending. The bees die off and are driven into the ground. Mysticism is a risky venture. I admit that there have been great mystics in the Christian tradition who have left intriguing works behind them. I also understand that the themes of mystics, as just outlined, are indispensable. Still, I cannot conceal the ambivalent feelings I have. Could it be that my fear as a Protestant that "the way above" or "the way inside" can be at odds with the lowly path which God himself undertook? Is it possible that spirituality also follows overly lonesome roads, searching for authentic religious experience and absolute transparency before God, that it despises the cloak worn by the deity himself? Is it possible that the way of emptying oneself can be a subtle form of pride? We need not answer these questions with a Yes or No. It's a sensitive question. In these matters,

God alone knows the hearts. In a Protestant setting, where the individual becomes an authentic individual, there lies a danger of concealed narcissism. That is not imaginary. In that situation, the guidance of a wise abbot can prevent a lot of trouble.

Frozen Faith

There is yet another shape of winter faith, one that is neither the end of faith, nor the faith of the mystic, but a prior form, that of a deeply hidden faith. It is the form in which faith lies, so to speak, frozen in the soul. This form is found in rigid orthodox thought movements. What began as an "inner gestalt" from Christendom has slowly but surely become sectarian. The focus on and ultimately excessive attention to the workings of the Spirit in the human heart, strange as it may seem, left the people in the cold. Placing the magnifying glass of the Spirit on the human heart resulted in myopia. The circle of true believers shrank to a few individuals who could then boast about the inner work of the Holy Spirit. This emphasis on the inner life which, through glossalia, almost expressed itself as a language of Canaan, became a system. A wall was put up, doors were closed, and the keys were put away. This happens especially where the doctrine of election not only placed the majority of people outside the church but also surrendered those inside the church to the cold of winter. Only a remnant of true believers remains. They dare to go to the table of the Lord. Standing around them are the others, shivering, awaiting the touching of their soul that will also give them access to the sanctuary. The adventure of the soul turns into a long period of waiting until the lot also falls on you, if it falls at all. All that remains is the form, increasingly rigid. A form which, after the stirring of the water stops, becomes an empty form. Even here, God seems to be dead. God is gone. Hidden in a few privileged souls. Outside, winter reigns.

Frozen souls, yes, but they can be thawed out. And as they thaw, the flowers can begin to bloom again. Here, too, through the love of the Lord, the thawed May water can perform wonders. The severe weather of an ecclesiastical culture relents as the sun begins to shine deep in the night and overcomes the cold. It is wrong, therefore, to dismiss these folk as if only the high and mighty deserve recognition. We can never tell when the Holy Spirit will erupt and find a lodging. And as the sun begins to shine and the flowers display their beauty, it happens often that they do so in hues of many-colored splendor.

The Boundaries of Winter Gestalt

The boundaries of the winter gestalt are breached whenever, on the grounds that God is silent, we cease to speak about God as well. Away with theology (except for the silent God), away with evangelism, away with the church.

There are shapes of theology which intentionally make God a concealed God. Those are forms in which by deliberate choice a so-called "negative theology" is proposed. God can be spoken about only in negatives, and to the extent that God is the wholly Other, he disappears from the world of human language and experience. God is so wholly, so unique, so different that he manifests himself only as the silence between two waves, as a chink in existence, as an opening in a gas pipe.

All this is sensitive and also meaningful language that certainly belongs to the vocabulary of God if it is to remain meaningful. At the same time a false note sneaks in whenever speaking about God is condemned as gibberish, the talk of children. If that were so, then only the prophets of negation are to be trusted with talk about God (or, as they would have it, the refusal to speak about God). These prophets absolutize their own role, as if God is only The Other of the so-called differential philosophers and theologians. Also, the plague of idolatry is promoted by silence. There is a form of silence that is essential. The "I lay my hand upon my mouth" of Job after God has spoken, and the "I hide my face" of Elihu after God appears in a still soft voice, cannot be ignored. If, however, we are obliged to be only silent before God, then eventually such silence becomes trite. Silence is the stillness between two waves. Without the voice of the waves, silence says nothing. It sometimes appears that pleading for silence about God is an attempt to lock him behind closed doors and is compatible with a secular attitude to life. Let God be silent, they say; we can live with that.

Summer Freckles in Winter

With this we have come to the frontiers of the winter shape of faith. Is it possible to have faith without the experience of winter? True, but we should not overdo it. God does have some rare children who walk daily in his light. They appear everywhere, even where you expect them the least. They are summer freckles in winter. They are like the strange but lovely Nepomuk in the darkly-laced *Doctor Faustus* by Thomas Mann. This book revolves around the fatal and tragic figure of Adrian, a musician, who appears on the eve of the Second World War. Nepomuk, a "butterfly" from God himself, even deeply disturbs Adrian, who is nearing the end of his life. As Nepomuk lies sick on his bed, which will prove to be his deathbed, the strange benedictions he pronounces are a comfort for all. One of the blessings he pronounces goes as follows: "Whoever lives according to God's laws, / Goodness is in him, and he is in God. / I entrust myself to him / For a good rest, since I am weary."[4] Nepomuk goes to sleep with these words every night until the last night, when he dies. Sons of God there will always be. Often they are "the poor in spirit." They are points of light in an often dark world.

The winter faith shape falls short of belief in God. One may not always experience God. But, then, is he *never* experienced? That would turn the scale much too far. Does the Spirit, then, really never do anything with our spirit? That is, however, the intent of the Spirit, though it is not forbidden to lend the Spirit a hand. For example, to speak this way about God, and honoring him in this way, will open the likelihood that your experience of God will become enlarged.

4. Mann, *Doctor Faustus*, 516.

6

Afterword

Faith and the Seasons
of the Soul

A Plurality of Seasons

I INTEND NOW TO look back briefly at what we have seen in this chapter's overview. In those passages we reviewed various faith forms. Faith is almost beyond our ability to describe. Its source is an open hand, man's receptiveness before God, man's Yes to God's Yes. But faith is not so naked that it does not become a garment for people of flesh and blood. Belief takes on distinct shapes. One hopes that the description of those forms brings the "invisible" faith a bit closer.

I have chosen four faith shapes, divided according to the seasons. These are not rigid distinctions, but they glide into each other and move in all directions. As has been said earlier, to make a sharp distinction among them is wrong. Moreover, what is important above all is to recognize that the differences are so great that they cannot be enclosed in just a foursome. The descriptions are approximations, stereotypes, attempts to put on paper at least something of the bird's eye overview.

Climate of the Soul

What these shapes have in common is that they draw a picture of the "climate of the soul," a metaphor in which soul stands for the spirituality of a person. Faith alters people. It brings them into an environment, a climate, which requires choice. Whether it is the young green of spring, the warmth of summer, the mist of autumn, or the ice of winter—similar things happen in man. The human soul becomes *climatological*. That happens because the soul does not exist in a vacuum. There is no human life that is not climatological. Does ground exist on its own? Ground that is stripped from the green layer of spring, from the cracks caused by the summer sun, from the fallen leaves of autumn, from the winter blanket of snow, ground that does not reflect anything, in which there is no push of fertility, ground on which no rains fall, devoid of atmosphere, on which no shadow falls from the clouds, over which no heavenly blue forms a canopy? Such ground is abstract ground, ground for the laboratory, ground in sacks. It is not living ground.

Similarly, can one reflect on the human soul just by itself? No. There is a climate of the soul. The soul is in constant motion. There are shapes, temperatures, emotions, promptings. Such is the human soul. It is not flat, empty, naked; it is not a laboratory soul. The soul is not a neutral entity. Man is immersed into a sphere, a circle of life. The human soul is a motley entity, varied. It is "gestalt-like." The one shape is richer than the other; there are leaner times and richer times. We human beings do not have dead souls and should watch out not to get them.

That awareness has always been there. It is the awareness of the notion that the soul can survive only when it is immersed in an atmosphere, initiated in a circle of life, trained for a culture of living and working. It remains to be seen whether this should always be a specific project. There was a time when this did occur. One thinks of the gymnasium and lyceum, institutions with a comprehensive program to shape a person by developing all his abilities and introducing him into the riches of (Western) civilization. That ideal has for the most part disappeared. That is a loss. It has known its grandeur and its misery, but it has been for the most part abandoned. Was it too elitist? Was it too proud of being "high culture," while looking down on the common folk? Was it a reminder of a classical world of harmonious personalities, no longer believed?

The question is this, what education ideal has come in the place of the classical ideal? One thinks of the emancipation model, or the model of self-development—ideals which may well be elitist as well but have a strong impact and serve more or less as functional norms. These models surely have power. They have an eye for the needs and aspiration of the individual. The weakness, however, is that the human being begins to detach himself from reality and loses contact with the real world. There is often the fear of attachment so that the person involved starts floating in a vacuum.

The question about climate of the soul is exciting. There is a general feeling that the soul lives in an impoverished atmosphere. Mere bread and games will leave the soul behind, empty. A human being is more than a drain of human experiences without even one of them enduring. Human life is more than a successful grazing of a meadow full of possibilities. The "more" is difficult to define, especially when traditional reference points are missing. We do our best to nourish or protect a child's soul with stories in the spring of life. And many grown souls wander foolishly in a New Age summer park. Are these adults really serious? Is it flirting? The soul sometimes, in desperation, searches for a climate, and the esoteric world of secret knowledge is an attractive candidate to provide it. Man cannot do without a climate, without images that fill his soul and let shadow and light fall upon it, in his more personal life as well as in the wider context, for we want to be clothed and not found naked (cf. 2 Cor 5:3). We want spring, summer, autumn, or winter, and fear a dead world with only artificial light and a climate controlled by technology.

God Gives Us the Seasons

Belief brings us in contact with God and with God's world. That's why faith influences man. It makes the soul, as already said, climatological. That has everything to do with the God in whom one believes. God is not detached, a metaphysical point without any relationship to life. Neither is he a God who tosses questions or strange wisdom which we are expected to believe, and then no longer affiliates with us. In the first section we spoke about the epic, lyrical, and dramatic categories of revelation. These epic, lyrical, and dramatic categories exist by the grace of an "epic, lyrical, and dramatic" God. The Christian faith is not a theory about a number of truths. It is even less a set of ideals. None of these make the soul climatological.

Belief in God is belief in God as Father, Son, and Holy Spirit. He is a God who gives life and imparts life. He is a God who resurrects man from the dead and puts him on the way of grace and righteousness. The Christian life is a matter of living from God, living in Christ, living through the Spirit.

It is belief in a God who appears to people on their journey and who offers peace to the weary and the heavy laden. Belief creates the seasons of the soul. That colors heart and soul and also touches the hands and the feet. It is faith in a God who is Spirit, creates freedom, causes restlessness, conjures up a vision, turns man into a pilgrim on the way to the eternal city, nurtures an inner world that is high, deep, and wide, and makes of that inner world one that shows itself in all its comings and goings.

The Western Adventure

Seasons do not occur everywhere in the world. In the tropics, monotony rules, with a climate hardly interrupted by monsoons. I have lived six years in the Smaragd (Indonesian archipelago) with great pleasure, but I missed the seasons.

The narrative of the seasons of belief as presented in the foregoing is a narrative out of the temperate zone of Europe. Not all Christians in this world encounter seasons as metaphors in the same way. What I have described is a typical account of Christian belief in the Western world. It is here that Christian faith has operated effectively over a long period of time. That faith became a partner of the culture which, in part, developed along with the growth of the Christian faith and in part turned against it. The result was a variety of forms of faith.

In other parts of the world, other forms of faith have developed where the metaphor of the four seasons probably is not as functional. The spectrum of Western Christian spirituality apparently is so uniquely diverse, existing nowhere else, that it already takes four words to describe something of its richness. That does not mean that the other forms are inferior, but they are different. A book about faith such as this is, in any case, a distinctively Western book.

PART 3

The Church

1

Introduction

The Church Is the Presupposition

WE HAVE SAID LITTLE about the church to this point. We have written generously about God and revelation. We have also extended our discussion to include belief and the faith contours of individual people. Perhaps the question has occurred to the reader just what place the church has in this great narrative. Has not the suggestion entered your mind that the proper theme is "God and the individual person," and that the church is merely an adjunct? Were I to assert this, I would not find myself in bad company. No one less than the church father Augustine proposed that "God and the Soul" is the proper concern for theologians.[1] It is also striking that in the older faith books no mention of church as a separate theme occurs. What is treated fully is the sacraments and sacred acts which occur within the church or proceed from the church, but that is something other than a chapter about the church.

I am of a mind, however, that in a faith book, we need to talk about the church. I must confess, in all honesty, that if there were not or has not been a church, and I did not myself did not constitute part of the church, I would have little to say about faith and revelation. In either case, this word from the church father Cyprian has some worth: "I would not have God as my Father if I did not have the Church as my mother." Freely interpreted, the

---

1. Augustine, *Soliloquies*, 18.

meaning is this: I would not know that God is my Father if I had not heard this from my mother, the church. The earlier faith story is not an expression of individual conviction. It is, true, an individual expression, but then from the belief that it has been handed to me through the church.

I have no authority to write what I have just asserted. I say, simply, and personally, that I derive my story from the tradition of the church. I would have little to tell about that belief if I were a person who lives merely as an individual before the face God. At a universal level, belief without the church becomes vague and narrow, and barely possible to compare it with the seasons. Unsung, if the church fades, it becomes moralistic. I would say further that in the narrative about the revelation of God, the church figures solidly. The church is not a human invention but an invention of God himself. God is indeed involved in a human community of brothers and sisters who share life together, and His revelation is therefore directed on it. That needs no discussion. The reader can reason that out for himself.

The Individual Has His Own Place

It remains true, nevertheless, that I did not begin with the church. That goes a little against the so-called *ecclesial turn*, the attitude toward the church which a number of theologians are propagating. I do not really object that strongly toward this turn. That will become apparent in this discussion of the church. As already stated, belief and revelation are left hanging without a connection to a faith community. That is not to deny that there is more than just the church. There is also the individual believer. Such a person may still belong to a church, but he is also himself. The believer needs the church, but the reverse is also true: the church needs the individual believer. Whenever the church becomes a social organization which allows no place for free individuals, then the church has become a forced community. And whenever worth and meaning of one's personal life becomes a collective matter, then we are dealing with a caricature of the church, and not with its true basis.

Everything is church, but church is not everything. I am still here, too. A true church does not become a "clammy" community, nor does it exist as a place where you are brainwashed. Rather, the church is there precisely to help the individual find his freedom, also as an individual believer. A strong church requires strong believers. And the reverse. A strong believer remains strong only when there is a strong faith community free of frivolous talk, but where the light of God's revelation may shine freely. A strong church remains strong only when there are grown-up believers who can stand on their own legs and who, if necessary, criticize the church.

I am well aware that I write as I do because I am a believer within the Western world. That world is the place where room has been made for the individual. In the Western world the axe has been set in the frozen lake of a collectivism which holds a person in its grip. And rightly so. I am convinced that this is an important achievement, one which had much to do with the impact of the Christian leaven. Its origins lie deeply rooted in the Bible and come through most clearly in Jesus and Paul. With Jesus it is the individual person whose soul and salvation are at stake. To a man who wished to be a follower of Jesus but protested that he must bury his father (as was a social and religious obligation) Jesus said, "Follow me, and let the dead bury their dead" (Matt 8:22). And Paul knew that he fell under the judgment of God, which permitted him to say, "To me it matters not at all if I am called to account by you or by any human court" (1 Cor 4:3). That did not make him an autonomous person. How could that be? Because, he writes, "the life I now live is not my life, but the life Christ lives in me" (Gal 2:20). It says, however, that Christ lives in *me*, and not only in the collective that is called the body of Christ.

Therefore, the idea that of the individual who is never completely subjugated is not per se an un-Christian idea. Even the idea of a lonely individual is not an un-Christian idea. Solitariness is all too readily labeled as a vice. Fortunately, there are people who, though of a solitary bent, do not on that account refuse to be part of the community. They can be the visionaries whom we desperately need. The renewing impulses of the church have often been originated by people who, without consciously promoting or cultivating this themselves, will not altogether simply accept the attitude of *comme il faut*, things as they should be. These are precisely the persons who introduced renewal to the church. Mature people, thus, fit well the idea of a Christian church constructively. And the reverse.

But there is also another side. The mature person who tries to demonstrate his individualism and who distances himself in this respect from tradition and fellowship, is weak. The true individual knows that the deepest relationship involves community. The truly self-reliant person is not ashamed to be, in a sense, provincial. It is the pseudo-independent people who seek their strength in opposing communities, and it is the pseudo-bohemians who flirt with their own independence and maladjustment.

We do not find such folk in the annals of history. Without traditions, and without carriers of tradition, not much will come of individual lives.

The popular idea that the Christians masses are so pitifully cut off from those folk who can think for themselves has been discredited, even though some still keep hammering on that anvil. Christians are often individuals in their own environments. They need the church even if for nothing more than as individuals who wish to keep a firm grip on their faith. And for all those who take pride in their ability to think for themselves and don't need the church, it turns out that they are disappointed when they try to do so. They often think along the same line. Often they disclose a provincial insularity toward church and faith, and they suffer from religious stress. People are by nature joiners, and even when they live outside living tradition and a lively fellowship, they often succumb hopelessly to the spirit of the age and the fashion of the day. In a church which is worthy of the name, you are not supposed to behave as a mere follower, nor as one who keeps an eye on the others. You will be told a story that exceeds your own. Moreover, you will have to accept that story. You must affirm it for yourself so that it becomes truly a part of yourself.

I have in the above discussion launched the theme of church for the purpose of describing the relationship of the individual to the community. That prepares us for the treatment of images about the church which I will present in the following chapter. I am aware that perhaps that may seem overworking the idea that the church is more than an essential prop for the individual. The church as community has its own identity. Even if I did not need the church to keep my faith vital, the church still has a substantial meaning. God knows every person as an individual, but it was said already in the beginning that it is not good for man to be alone (Gen 2:18). Human beings are not intended to exist as monads, but as members of a community. God himself is not a monad, but a fellowship of Father, Son, and Holy Spirit. That fellowship is reflected in the community of human beings. The deliverance is not a deliverance of discreet persons who will be saved individually. The goal of history lies in the reconciliation between God and man and among people mutually. The church on earth begins that narrative.

2

Images of the Church

WHOEVER CONTEMPLATES WRITING A book about faith must, sooner or later, write about the church. The Christian faith did not begin as a world view of individual believers but took the form of communal living. The Holy Spirit was poured out upon all flesh. What remained in the wake of the stormy Pentecost visitation after it had passed was a fellowship of brothers and sisters united in the name of Christ. What began then, has continued. Today the church is a worldwide church.

There is no reason to complain about the countless books that have addressed the theme of the church. Frequently they fuse with the theme of the future. The reason for this boom is that things are not going well with the church—at least, the church in our part of the world. Thus, for obvious reasons, we are prompted to think about the church of the future. What goes well, what can be improved, but, above all, how can it be otherwise? Alongside this, the practice of therapy comes into play. The views point in a variety of directions, so that it is impossible that all of them can be effective. Time, we say, will teach us how the church will fare. Time is a sieve, through which all sorts of initiatives pass, and on which, fortunately, what is useful remains. Useful, also, for the Holy Spirit who "trekt met heel zijn kerk van land tot land als God's Gezant" (moves with healing over his church from land to land as God's envoy; *Liedboek voor de kerken*, 304:3). Whenever the church faces a crisis, one may expect that all that is written about that crisis and proposed solutions are also itself part of that crisis.

I am convinced that we in the church need to ask the question, What are we doing in the church? before we busy ourselves about the future of the church and seek ways to overcome the crisis. A problem with today's church is that we are often confused about the why of the church, why it is necessary now. Van Ruler calls it "a booth on the market of life" (een tent op de markt van het leven). The answer to the question why the tent must exist and must remain, however, seldom receives an answer. Often church folk themselves hardly make clear for themselves and others what purpose a church serves. They often do little more than look after each other (omzien naar elkar). Without an answer to the question of the need for the church, even the salvific purpose of the church, it makes no sense to have a discussion about the church and the future. Giving the church a facelift is quite meaningless if we don't even know what a church is for and how to handle it.

Because of the frequent vagueness or lack of clarity about what happens in the church and what we are looking for in it, I am looking for places where people gather with a clear idea of what is going on. It is all about "institutions" that are more or less necessary and that engage the question of what it means to be human. It is about places whose purpose for existence is clear. If we go there, we know why. We know what they can do for us. The search has to do with places where this meaning is clear. As we identify these places, we should know why. We will know what the church promises us.

Some of these places will provide us with an explanation of what the church is about, namely, as a place where something is really happening, something that actually affects our humanness. That you will find yourself borrowing from left and right is no problem. Even an image such as "body" existed already before Paul used it to describe the church. In that respect the authors of the Bible were very frank. Thus, it is acceptable for us now to look for relevant and revealing images, even if they are not used all that much in the church. Of course, at some point comparisons fail us. It is thus a matter of making do with the images we have. The church is unique, and does not, at its very heart, let itself be compared with anything or anybody. The church is a creation of the Spirit; it is the body of Christ himself. Thus, the metaphors can be only somewhat helpful. It is only after attaining this sharper insight (nut en noodzaak, value and need of the church) that we can start reflecting on the future of the church again.

The first image I choose to use is that of a hospital. The second is the theater. The third is a parliament. The fourth is the temple. That one, the temple, can hardly be called an image, since it is nearly identical to the church itself. But I believe the differences are sufficiently great to cast light upon the church.

Not all places where people assemble are equally suitable as metaphors for the church. The entity *Supermarket* presented itself, but was soon dismissed. I have no quarrel with people in the church who look for something that suits their taste, but that criterion itself is too minimal to serve as a true representation of the church. On the contrary, the church as a supermarket turns the gospel into a reduced price item, and the gospel will not permit that. I lingered longer over church as a business, but finally rejected that, mindful of the saying, "It dies a death by a thousand qualifications." True, the church has similarities with a business: people come together to do something that is useful for others. However, through such a metaphor the church would actually appear too much like work, and like an organization, which would mean the loss of the essence of the church. The church as a lodge, meanwhile, has gained prominence, but I need not recapitulate that here. The church as court room, as a community center, as a tavern, and as a sport school I find intriguing and fitting for further comparison. But since I intend to limit my metaphors to four, these others have fallen off the boat. Moreover, broadly speaking, especially these four images cover important aspects of human life: that of health and health care, of culture, of politics, and that of religion.

The four metaphors I will consider are based on reality. They are the church as it actually exists in the real world. I am inventing nothing new. At the same time, they are images meant to remind us of something. True, often the church is not any more than this. That is no calamity. The church rattles at all sides and is often not what it should be. The four metaphors are therefore not intended to make the church live up to what it ideally should be. That would simply paralyze the effort. The metaphors are intended as *triggers* which half describe, half prompt, memory. They are, as I have stated, especially meant to offer an idea of what one can expect in the church and why a church is necessary as "its own booth on the market of life." In that respect, they are meant as a reminder of what the church is, something that often gets snowed under or forgotten. Just as true, in one faith community one image will become more prominent, and in another, a different image. I also think the four images need each other as they mutually refer to and define each other. It would be an illusion to assume that they exist as a complete set in every faith community. Who can have everything in his home anyway?

3

The Church as Hospital

THE CHURCH AS HOSPITAL is an ancient metaphor. It has fallen out of use, but it deserves a second life. On first sight it does not appear an attractive metaphor. It calls up associations that the church and the sick are to be flung together on a heap, and confirms the idea that the church and the ill belong together. On closer examination, however, illness is not shameful, and the hospital is not only for the pathetically sick. We are all aware how fragile is health, and at great risk, so that a hospital stay becomes necessary. The advantage of the metaphor is that it appears that the church is not a luxury for healthy and thriving people. I have consequently chosen to lead with this metaphor for that reason. Why do we need a church? Because you are ill, and because you do not wish to remain so.

In a hospital, you are a patient. You undergo an operation there. You receive treatment, and you swallow medicine. The hospital proposes a regimen that you are expected to follow. In a hospital there are doctors who operate on you and nurses around taking care of you. They have more knowledge about operations and medicine than you do, and, therefore, you consent to lay your fate in their hands. You hope they will make you better, and, fortunately, that occurs often. The idea of a hospital is that you are ill when you arrive, but, thankfully, through treatment, you do not remain ill. You are made healthy again, or so healthy that you can move forward again. In that case, a hospital is, for example, different from a rehabilitation site, and surely different from a hospice.

The modern hospital is a highly complex institution. With its origin in a Christian culture, where caring for the sick was regarded as one of the seven works of charity, it has now often developed into a secular and highly professional institution with a complex culture. I shall not pursue these complexities any further. I shall limit myself to the basic ideas I describe above, the ideas which arise spontaneously whenever people hear about a hospital. Does my outlining these basic ideas of a hospital prompt a recognizable profile which can clarify for you what happens in a church? Does it help us to discover something new about the church?

The Sick and Sinners

To portray the church as a hospital assumes that we are dealing with spiritual health. Jesus said, "It is not the healthy who need a doctor, but the sick" (Mark 2:17). The sick which Jesus had in mind were such folk as Zacchaeus and Levi, tax collectors, who were ostracized by the elite of the day. Moreover, Jesus also attracted faithful followers, but also a variety of "truly" sick people. Wherever Jesus appeared, he gathered all sorts of folk from every corner and burg, imploring him to heal them. Also, the demon-possessed approached Jesus, and he cast the evil spirits out. Jesus was not surrounded by the perfectly healthy men and women. Rather, they were a mess of irregular people, an assemblage of faltering and sick people. When he comes to a place, he has them sit on the grass, and the people listen to what he has to say. He sees them as sheep without a shepherd, leading purposeless lives. Jesus is concerned about the fate of these people. We find, surrounding Jesus, an intense awareness of one's own sickness, with one's own private burdens and emptiness, one's own spiritual hunger and thirst.

What the gospels record is not intended as mere historical information. This is how the world around Jesus appears: many weary and burdened folk. The church which grows out of this situation is far from home. Whenever the church becomes a community of spiritually healthy people, well-fed, all good people, successful people, among whom anyone who does not dare approach them is not truly welcome, then the cause of the gospel is betrayed. Perhaps the following passage from a novel by Dostoevsky can serve as a warning. It is a monologue from a figure of the type frequently found in his novels. The monologue has the ring of all self-pitying and pathetic creatures; still, it is a voice not so different from the words Jesus spoke about those who do not need a doctor:

It was tribulation I sought . . . tears and tribulation, and I have found it and I have tasted it; but He will pity us who had pity on all men, who has understood all men and all things, He, the One . . . He too is the judge. He will come in on that day and he will ask, "Where is the daughter who gave herself for her cross, consumptive step-mother and for the little children of another? Where is the daughter who had pity on the filthy drunkard, her earthly father, undismayed by his beastliness?" And he will say, "Come to me! I have already forgiven thee once . . . Thy sins are many which I forgive thee, for thou has loved much." . . . And I will forgive my Sonia. He will forgive me, I know it . . . I felt it in my heart when I was with her just now! And he will judge and forgive all, the good and the wise and the meek . . . And when he has done with all of them, then he will summon us, "You too come forth, ye drunkards, come forth, come forth you weak ones, children of shame and shall stand before them." And he will say unto us, "Ye are swine, made in the image of the Beast and with his mark but come ye also!" And the wise ones and those of understanding will say, "O Lord, why dost thou receive these men?" And he will say, "This is why I receive them, oh ye of understanding, that not one of them believed himself worthy of this." . . . And he will hold out his hands to us and we shall fall down before him . . . and we shall weep . . . and we shall understand all things.[1]

Admittedly, this passage inclines toward the pseudo-romantic. We live in the Netherlands and not in tsarist Russia. The church consists of ordinary people and not an assembly of drunkards. Still, it would be unfortunate if the church denies a place for people whose lives are at loose ends. The church is a place for the respectable, but also for less respected people, for the civilized and the less civilized, for the righteous and the wise (surely!) but also for sinners and fools. The church is a point of contact for physically healthy people, but also for invalids and people mentally and physically ill. It cannot be otherwise. The sphere of the complacent who sneak into almost every community is challenged by the proclamation of the gospel, which points toward people who need the gospel. A proclamation, then, must distance itself from the moralism of an old-fashioned or modern school-master type with his "Johnnie once saw plums hanging, looked at them, and still let them hang." It is the proclamation of a God who raises the dead and promises life to dying people. And if the proclamation should return to moralism, the celebration of the Eucharist will bring an

1. Dostoevsky, *Crime and Punishment*, 25–26.

end to that. Jesus Christ appears as the resurrected Lord for people who need him. Bread and wine, body and blood of Christ, get distributed to those who hunger and thirst. Salvation lies in a lacerated body. It does not lock anyone out, and invites everyone in.

Self-Encounter

Illness gives a patient a private encounter with himself. One who is healthy finds it easier to flee from himself than one who is ill. An ill person is thrown back upon himself. There are enough healthy believers who can flee from themselves and escape to an ideal world. A proclamation to healthy people concerning this and that which is needed and useful, may still not about you. Why should it be about you? What ails you, then? One who is really sick in the sense that Jesus means has himself at stake. It is all about me, says this sick person.

It is precisely here that Christian faith begins. That is not, this time, about one or another theory concerning society, and the improvement of mankind or the world, or speculation over signs of hope (but were we really that close to despair?). The Danish Kierkegaard was right in his opposition to the speculative philosophy of Hegel, when he questions self-concern: "Betting totally on yourself in the concern for yourself."[2] The truth is subjective, he wrote later. What he meant is that truth is existential truth and is concerned with our deepest self. Self-concern is something other than you circling about yourself or being busy with your own project. It has to do with what Jesus said, "What does anyone gain by winning the whole world at the cost of his life?" (Mark 8:36). It is a matter of coming to yourself," as described in the parable of Jesus about the lost son: "Then he came to himself" (Luke 15:17). After his self-alienation in a far land there occurred in his life a moment of self-reflection and repentance.

Being ill throws you back upon yourself. Whenever the church is a hospital, it means that you need also to come to yourself. It means also that you need to be worked on. You do not come to the church first of all to be drilled in the doctrine of the church, nor to develop some vision of the world and the future. These surely have their place, but not at the cost of ignoring yourself. There is involved in all this a *matter of ultimate concern*, and that is yourself. Heeding Christ in the community of believers

2. Kierkegaard, "Das Buch Adler," 483.

indicates that you need "Arts Aller Zielen" (Healer of all souls; *Liedboek voor de kerken*, 170:2).

> The dripping blood our only drink,
> The bloody flesh our only food:
> In spite of which we like to think
> That we are sound, substantial flesh and blood
> Again, in spite of that, we call this Friday good.
> (T. S. Eliot, "Burnt Norton")

The church is the place for honesty. Anyone going to the hospital does not go there to report how well things are with him. Truth on the sick bed is being preferred to imploring gestures of a doctor. We are not "sound of flesh and blood," however we like to prop up our well-being. The illusion is taken from us. This is not a tragedy. There is "a wounded surgeon" and "the healer's art" (ibid.). He knows how to give counsel to the sick. He also has the skill to name illnesses. It is a liberation whenever the pathology, the root of the disease, is identified and the poisonous ground of our concealed thoughts and the crippling "anxieties and worries" exposed which cover the soul and stifles life.

However much we are called to be concerned about our neighbor, this is not the place for that, but rather to prompt you to stand before the mirror and repent of your ways. The church is specifically designed to deal with man's relationship to God, and through that relationship with the neighbor and the world. When the last becomes disconnected from the first, the church loses its unique theme and simply repeats what can mostly be better said elsewhere. I fear for the neighbor and the world that they will not find pleasure in the miseries of people who are ablaze with moral health. I even think that there is nothing more annoying than just that. The church must not, in any case, become a club where everyone is happy, full of beaming people, where all sing in a major key, and where no tears flow. Such people we are not, and the church is not the place to talk each other into that.

Living with Illness and Mortality

One comes to a hospital in order to regain his health. That can happen only through good treatment, perhaps through an operation, often through medication. Jesus compares himself to a physician who has come to bring healing to people. He did that, literally. He healed the lame, the blind, the deaf, the dumb, the crippled, the feverish, the leper. He freed people from evil spirits. He even raised individuals from the dead. For a short time the kingdom of God was trembling with excitement around the Sea of Galilee, perhaps a year, maybe three years. After that the movement concentrated into a luminous site around the cross. It accompanied Jesus through the night of Golgotha and appeared with him in the garden of the resurrection. After that came the church.

For many, all this is a great disappointment. Where has the stirring power of the kingdom of God remained? The answer is that it is easing, and we just have to cope with it. Enough spirits have come since who would willingly rouse the storm once more. Think of Jan van Leiden, who would liberate the world from tyranny. Think also of today's faith healers who pretend they can heal (almost) all diseases. These, however, are just illusions. The early wine of the kingdom has matured. The sick lie abed longer, and many must wait until the day of resurrection. Every community has to deal with that. That is also true for the community that was "hallmarked" by the church.

For the sick we have hospitals, doctors, and medicine. The kingdom of God arrived and the hospitals sprang up. Sometimes somebody is healed without all that; this may be a remarkable sign and as a proof that God does not always draw the lines according to the normal patterns. Moreover, some sick people will not be cured, but who will receive good care. Next to *cure* is *care*. That can also happen in the church. Prayers are offered for the sick. Visitors call, and flowers are brought. (If this has happened to you, you know whereof I speak.) Some sick receive anointing with oil. Should a patient die, grieving takes place for the dead, and the relatives are shown kindness and compassion. All these things are done in the faith that Jesus knows about our suffering and that these things are important. Such gestures often bring healing, even though the patient does not get better. No *cure*, but *care*. That applies not only to the physically but also to the mentally ill. Therapy for depression may not be offered, but brothers and sisters are familiar with the situation. It is all this which is the unique character of the church as a faith community. Man is a vulnerable being, but he is part of a community. And this helps as well for the well-being of the soul. Depression is pervasive, but studies show that faith and a church fellowship in such situations often have a positive influence on such folk.

Not everyone is ill. It is true that something is always rattling, and that will continue until our death. Either way, we are mortal, and we are ignorant of the day of our death. The idea of a life of good health concluding with a good pension that allows for ample enjoyment is wrongheaded.

The hidden thought is that death can be shunted off to the side in the belief "that we can finally get out of life alive."[3] One must sometimes challenge such mistaken notions, though without succumbing to depression. In place of an ideal world of only healthy people who have a good handle on their lives, there is a real world of vulnerable people, with mortal bodies and a spirit not made of steel.

That is the sort of people we are, and that is how we live before the face of God. We know about the royal day which revelation tells us about (Rom 8:18), and still, until that time, we groan in ourselves, in expectation of the revelation that we are children of God (8:23). That does not reduce us to pathetic creatures but into people who learn perseverance and cultivate courage. Courage is a vulnerable virtue. Sometimes it is right in the hospital that people acquire surprising courage. Courage is sown in the church as a hospital, and for people who are not fire-eaters but who are still learning to live out the life of faith.

And whether we are sick or well, we must all die. The great taboo about death is overcome in the church as hospital. That is liberating. We will leave this world dead, not alive. However accurately we have fastened all our buttons and however healthy we may have been, this is the pivot on which everything finally turns. There are no herbs or medicines for the dead. The only help the dead now have is the violent outburst of the resurrection. It is not coincidental that the Christian community worships on the same day that Jesus rose from the dead. That is because though we hear the violent outburst at a distance, we are still alive.

Medicine

There is no such thing as perfect health. Perfect spiritual health even less so. That is not to say that, spiritual beings that we are, we have to resign ourselves to sickness. The church is not a place for resignation. It is the site of God's therapy. This can occur gently, almost invisibly, but can also take place as shock therapy. Anyway, something must happen with us. We are not programmed to leave life the same as we came into the world. We need, once we were born, to be baptized by water and the Spirit (John 3:5). We have need of God, and Christ, and the Holy Spirit, which renews us. The church has been designated to serve this purpose. Too often church is the place where we hear that it is God's profession to forgive, and that all

3. Hauerwas, *Working with Words*, 160.

good things will flow from that, as if that is the only message that should be communicated to us. Too often the church is a place for reflections that have nothing to do with us. Too often the church has become a place where nothing is required of you and where you do not need treatment. The mask of self-sufficiency which this situation prompts is stifling.

The age-old remedy which the church has extended is "Word and Sacrament." The Bible is a therapeutic book. Its purpose is not to remake us, but to renew us. The Bible, in other words, is intended to become a living word, one that releases us from our sickly inclinations and the toxic gods of the age. It is not a book that flatters, but one that places the finger on the wound. It is at the same time a book of healing; the pages of the Bible are as healing leaves on the wound of the soul. An entire library of devotional literature has dealt with this theme.

We shall never make progress if we neglect this function of the Bible. The Bible has been laid out systematically before us by responsible exegetes, and with good fortune our eyes are opened for the different layers in the Bible. But where is the sword that pierces the heart, where is the steel "that questions the distempered part"? (T. S. Eliot, *Four Quartets*, "East Coker"). Is there no sickness anymore? Or no more steel? Proclamation serves then to conceal reality (including of the soul) so that while Scripture is intended for another purpose, it now camouflages matters.

Next to the Bible and the gospel proclamation, the church provides opportunity to observe the Last Super, the Eucharist. To Christians of an earlier era, this was "medicine from immortal regions." The medicine is bread and wine through which we participate in the body and blood of Christ. It is medicine bitter and sweet at the same time. The price of the medicine was the very life of the Prince of Peace. And we who partake of this sacrament become one with a body that has died. The medicine aims at the death of the "old man," the man living outside faith, hope, and love. Only in this way do we provide entrance to the "new person." It cures us from the false deities and routs the demons. "You cannot drink the cup of the Lord and the cup of demons. You cannot partake of the Lord's table and the table of demons" (1 Cor 10:21). Nevertheless, it is also sweet medicine. It is after all medicine from immortal regions. It connects us not alone with the dead, but also with the life of Christ. It prepares the way for the power and life of the Holy Spirit.

Men's existence and Christian existence is a lifelong recovery process. For that reason, the regular practice of this medicine becomes an urgent necessity. Whenever the sacrament, by itself, expresses the mutual fellowship of believers, it can hardly be called the work of medicine. Whenever the signs of the bread and wine are not explicitly bound up with Christ, with his death and resurrection, then the practice becomes disconnected from the art of healing and becomes powerless or redundant.

As already stated, the church receives no chapter in the older doctrinal statements. True enough, the Apostles' Creed includes the "I believe a holy Catholic Church." Not much more gets said about the church. Thomas Aquinas, in his *Summa,* has little to say explicitly about the church, but he did write extensively about the sacraments. Only in the time of the Reformation was it seen as necessary to reflect directly about the church, because the split was *about* the church. Obviously, the theme of church governance and how authority was to be regulated was a *hot issue.* Still, under the heading The Church, the dominant themes were preaching and the sacraments. These were the means designated by the church to serve the believers in their faith-formation. About the church as a "social body" we hear little until the nineteenth century. Prior to this, the church was primarily "a sacred institution."

This may seem one-sided, especially since the word *institut* makes its appearance, but the "service of the Word and Sacrament" also has that aspect in it. It asks for an organization, and for people who are destined to play a role in it. If that does not happen, then it becomes a noncommittal play. I believe that the function of the church as an institution of salvation comes closest to clarifying why it is necessary. There is much in that institution that is not right, some of it sheer misery, but, still, we may not refuse it. Twenty centuries of wisdom about this medicine are embedded in this institution. It has been for twenty centuries the site where Christ has established himself, from hand to mouth, and I honestly do not know where more intensive drama has transpired than here.

Discipline

Word and Sacrament do not stand by themselves. They function in a liturgy. They are part of the life of the church. The church does not impose on anyone, but that does not mean it can be understood as an entity without engagement. There is what is called ecclesiastical discipline. That is a regimen intended to serve the spiritual health of its members. Discipline comes into play, for example, when punishment becomes necessary. As is well known, in the Roman Catholic Church this ritual comprises one of the sacraments. The Reformation Church took a different stance. It all revolved around misuse of the sacraments (think of the practice of indulgences). Unfortunately, what it really stands for is one thing; in practice the whole notion of penalty and forgiveness has become invisible. Voices are crying out for changes. "Confession and absolution are comparable to a treatment."[4] It would be worthwhile to remove confession and absolution from the dingy atmosphere of dingy meanings, followed by a perfunctory "I absolve you." Confession provides a sanctuary to speak about matters that must not be concealed, a place where the sinner can begin anew through the power of the word of forgiveness. It provides an ear which you can trust and a man who in God's name announces your forgiveness.

This involvement of the church is based on freedom, but freedom is not without engagement. He who prefers that no one intrude into his affairs must know that for himself. He who knows he is ill but prefers to treat himself with homemade remedies must also know that for himself. There is, however, an institution in this world that asserts that you can run into danger with makeshift palliatives which underestimate the seriousness of the disease and, therefore, do not help.

It is not that the church itself provides the medicine. God alone can help us, but God is not an abstract spirit. The Word has become flesh, or, in that connection, has become medicine. Word and sacrament and discipline are the means urgently needed, given the wretched moral state in which we find ourselves.

It is for that reason that the means God has placed at our disposal are to be used communally. They function well especially in a circle of believers in Jesus joined to the body of Christ. It could probably have been arranged some other way, but I will not pursue that now. This, however, needs a fellowship that knows that it is the bearer of these means. The church's use of the mother as metaphor is an old one, but it should be a mother who raises children, and not one who in the name of relaxed upbringing refuses to stretch her hand in order to keep her children from becoming undisciplined believers.

Becoming Cured

Do we recover in the hospital which we call church? That is a delicate question. God is busy with us. The Holy Spirit is not just an idea, but an *actor*.

4. Boer, "Kunnen Protestanten zonder de Biecht?" 264.

Whenever the church is compared with a hospital, it is for the purpose of shaping us. For that reason the church is a place for action and even of treatment. If the treatment yields no results, it means there was nothing on which to build. But surely we can expect some progress toward recuperation. Church discipline has some effect. By medicine and treatment, we may expect some rehabilitation. It is fruitless to listen to those who are suspicious about the possibility of growth. The letter writers of the New Testament assumed that growth does take place and that progress happens on the road of sanctification. The church is not a place where we simply read a lesson or turn a disk, but a place which helps healing. Healing from what? From unbridled conduct, crooked ways, from traumas, from prejudice, from depression, and, above all, from godlessness.

At the same time, it is clear that no one will be discharged from the hospital before his death. That would constitute a strange image. In the church, the people who support each other, who live alongside each other, who together make use of the means of grace, who even go outside the church to assist those who no longer feel the need of a church, will be exalted to royal status, and we will hardly count them among our dead. Above all, what does healing mean except having an eye and a heart for each other, and to live in the name of Jesus in love for each other, and to help bear each other's burdens? And where can you learn to do this more intensively and more effectively than in the church?

Thus, the church as hospital is a metaphor, not less, but not more either. No smell of disinfectants will be found in the church, and the people do not lie waiting for an infusion. Above all, the church as hospital is not the only metaphor. The church is also a theater, and a banquet hall. The church is a square where the private streets are well laid out and where you can walk and talk. But the church as hospital cannot be overlooked either. We are sick, and we search for healing, and we must already in this life begin the process of recovery. For that, you need the church.

4

The Church as Theater

THE METAPHOR OF CHURCH as theater has a close link with the section entitled "Dramatic." There we compared the world to a stage on which unique productions get performed. The role the human being plays in the production is connected to his daily life. That remains as it is. That cannot succeed, however, without a separate platform. That is the church. The church is also theater.

A theater requires actors and an audience. It needs productions to be performed, based on a text. There is a stage manager who oversees how the designated scrip gets executed on the stage. A great deal more can be said about the theater, but I will forego discussing such matters any further.

The metaphor of church as theater is not immediately obvious. Considering the long, wearying, strained relations between church and theater, that is not surprising. Over the familiar rubric "the broad and the narrow way," the theater is always positioned on the broad way. The critical attitude of Christendom toward the theater goes back to Roman times. The quality of the theater makes that understandable. Since then, the restrictive attitude toward the theater has for the most part disappeared. There is questionable theater, just as there are bad films, but that is not inherent in the medium. There is also good theater. Thus, it is appropriate to point out the many ways in which theater and church are comparable. Why do you go to church? Because it is good theater. And because a good production is being enacted.

The Production

What production, then, is being performed? It is the story of God's relationship with the world, which runs from the beginning of history to its end. In the middle stands Christ himself. In the section on the dramatic, we sketched out the main lines. That part is the particular focus of the church. That narrative is shown over and over again, from a variety of angles, and the hearers are invited to participate in it. The performance in the church is done with the intention, among others, of performing it outside the church as well. Other things are also done in the church, but this is what it really is about. If these essentials do not stand at the very center, the church gets lost, the worship service gets lost, the very essence of the church's being gets lost. It is impossible, of course, for the entire production to be performed. It is only a fragment of the complete production to which we are invited to attend. It gets elucidated. But it is a fragment of God's production. When this is not the case, the exciting center is gone. The church and the church service become non-committal, which causes them to focus on the merely interesting, the merely witty, the traditional, but nothing of consequence occurs.

Everything that happens in the church is founded on the narrative of God. One needs to see the performance. One must hear it. Again and again. You are invited to participate in it, for it is a narrative that is still going on. Involvement is liberating and healing. You become swept up in it. You sing along, you pray along, you listen, and watch, you eat and drink, you receive and give.

In our daily living we find ourselves involved in any number of mini-dramas, and we play a role in them all. If we do not understand the larger drama of God, however, those pieces have little meaning, and our lives often become melancholy, mere air and emptiness. In the middle of these mini-dramas, the production of God is being performed. The theme is the divine love which became flesh and blood. This is the high drama which proves endlessly fascinating. It gives meaning to our lives. It also enables us to participate in the other roles in daily life. Sometimes it reinforces our belief in our only comfort. Sometimes it inspires us to act with heightened enthusiasm. And we do that all with an eye on the script of God himself. We view the whole world as a stage on which God is carrying out his will, so that nothing we do falls outside his purview.

In order to persevere and retain our perspective, we need a separate stage of the church and of the liturgy of the church. That is where we get to see and hear God's high drama. That is where we ourselves became part of it. We participate and we practice our role.

Church Service as Spectacle?

Understandably, questions arise immediately. Is there a *public* when the church becomes a theater? When the congregation assembles, you can't very well address it as an esteemed public, can you?

Undeniably, this is often the way it has come through, especially in the established churches. The church-goers came together and saw what was happening at the liturgical center, the spot where a leader and eventually others performed. The other folk would sit on stools or benches; they were the spectators. In a Roman Catholic service one could easily get that idea, seeing a priest who, along with acolytes, performed the Eucharistic activities. In the worst case, it became a show of "for you" but "without you." The priest would mumble his "hocus pocus," a mistaken understanding of "Hoc est corpus meum" (This is my body). It was an idea of course far removed from the official liturgical doctrine, but, apparently, often the actual practice.

The Protestants were of a mind to break with this practice, preferring to make the spectators participants. In either case no drama emerged in the protestant churches. Faith always comes by hearing. Still, it cannot be denied that in the public worship the doctrine being elucidated would often be dramatized in the auditorium by a rhetorical creation, one that the church-goers should assess. This practice also stood at some distance from the teaching, but it nevertheless occurred. What is clear is that all this differed from what you would describe as a worship service.

A church service in that context can also become a spectacle, and that can still happen. Nowadays this development can come in the form of a highly polished performance, with accomplished actors, arranged to the finest detail, and enacted before an audience that needs to be entertained. All that, however, does not have much to do with true worship. In a genuine worship service the congregation is at least asked to participate in the program so that it becomes a communal undertaking.

Services Which Attract Interested Spectators

A church service is not a show. But should we, then, write off the whole idea of a show, in public, and with spectators? I am of a mind to deny that we must do this. Church folk form a mixed fellowship. Among them, there is a place for spectators. It would be uncharitable to compel everyone to participate or play an active part. There are also onlookers. One would hope that there are people who merely drop in to watch from a distance what there is to see and hear. One would even hope that such folk receive a hearty welcome without being immediately hugged to death. Of course, the idea is to turn spectators into participants, but that goes better with one than with another, and with some it will never occur. There is a place in the church for the auditor. For the time being this person comes to listen and look at what is happening. Young people will be there, with their parents, who themselves will not yet have made up their minds. They are people who show interest and who have walked into a church either by invitation from others, or spontaneously.

A church service is not a show. One hopes, however, that it is more than an arid production. When this occurs, it cannot be blamed on a lack of rhetorical skill of the pastor, let alone actor talent. It has, however, to do with the lack of a *sense of urgency*, and, with it, no awareness that what happens in church is really about to be, or not to be, about the real issues of life. A good play is about *tua res agitur*—experiences that have to do with your own daily life. Even though you cannot experience everything and be present at all that goes on, you would know that here, on this stage, something of interest is going on, and that something crucial is at stake. This must be obvious for the spectators of a church service.

That church services lack eloquence can also have as its cause the forms that are used. The parts that are sung may be so unfamiliar to a younger person that he may need a dictionary to enable him to sing. The church music needs to be appropriately chosen, but it must not give the slightest hint that it *swings*. The church service is painfully slow. I realize that the solution is not to catapult a musical combo into the church, or a still more amusing strategy, or entertaining the children with some small talk, or procuring another technologically savvy minister. Yet, these strategies matter, and it is no shame to reckon with a young and new audience.

A church service is a happening. It may be a dramatic scene, a moving production, breathtaking, surprising, because we are watching—and participating in—an exhilarating piece that touches us to the core. Dullness is a mortal sin. Better a sermon in which the preacher goes over the line of right teaching than a dull sermon. Better a liturgical adaptation where questions are raised at crucial points than a correct liturgy without any life or movement. A church service is a happening.

The border line between a spectator and a participant is fluid. A too great emphasis on an "alternative community" in which everyone participates and in which characters are shaped individually (as someone like Hauerwas advocates) places too much stress on people's consciences. Someone like Augustine would have, a long time ago, been harried out of the church. Fortunately, he could have stayed as a listener. Then, one day, he came under the spell of the preaching of St. Ambrose. Make certain that you keep a space for such Augustinians. But let there be Ambroses as well who have things to say to worldly folk and pleasure-seekers as they go through life. A church needs to have some semblance of a tent that is put up with the invitation to the neighborhood. Have a look at this. Listen to this.

Membership

This does not mean that one may remain a spectator indefinitely. The fact remains that remaining a spectator is ultimately incompatible with the divine drama. The tax collector Zacchaeus who wished to see Jesus with his own eyes when he came by was ordered to get out of the tree where, for a ten cent piece he could have a seat in the front row and become an actor in the drama (Luke 19:1–10). According to the Pharisees, he was a controversial player, but, fortunately, they were not in charge.

A moment about membership arrives. Now you, from being an observer, become a participant. That requires an initiation. You have learned a great deal about the art of performing by doing, but, more, and especially, you learn about the deep meaning of the production. Actually, you have busied yourself all your life about becoming a member, but this does not take away the fact that you have now reached a point of decision—whether or not to become a participant.

For a long time this joining was marked by baptism. In baptism you became incorporated into the body of Christ and a participant in the theater group of Christ. Baptism by its very nature is a unique type of drama. Through the water of baptism you bury your old life and receive a new one. Baptism is both death and resurrection. You are being mangled through the door of self-denial. There is hardly a more dramatic action conceivable than baptism. That drama runs right through you and plays out in the circle of brothers and sisters who have also undergone this ritual.

If you were baptized as an infant, a moment comes when you need to take responsibility for the baptism, a conscious acceptance of it usually called "Profession of Faith." When you do this, you are identifying yourself with the moment of baptism that you underwent before you were aware of it. A difference exists among churches whether baptism of children, even more of infants, can have any meaning. I respect those who advocate baptism at the time of the profession. The radical nature of baptism comes to expression at such times. The churches of Rome and of the Reformation both permit baptism of infants and children, particularly because of the belief that they, too, have a role in God's drama. "From the mouths of babes and infants at the breast, You have established a bulwark against your adversaries, to restrain the enemy and the avenger," says Psalm 8, somewhat militarily, but it is clear that also these voices are echoing the script of God. This goes to show that the performance is not designed only for believers of eighteen years and older.

This, however, is not a denial of the fact that we are talking about intentional members. In the absence of such a moment, you are suspended between spectator and actor, and that is too much "neither fish nor fowl." That was a complaint against what for a long time was called the national church—that too many people had settled into this border region.

Things are not well when in the church the moment of joining becomes relativized or kept vague. This can happen when being a Christian is relativized through the knockdown argument that you can be a good man outside the church also. That last is true, though the word "also" betrays a defensive posture. Becoming a Christian means surrender, and being "good" implies especially a deep yearning for God and a desire to serve him with one's whole heart and your neighbor as yourself. That is a real transitional point toward a new life, and, therefore, nothing must be permitted to detract from the radical choice of becoming a Christian and joining yourself to the body of Christ. Force is anger. This choice can have authenticity only when it is freely made. That puts matters strongly, but we are talking about making a choice with integrity.

In order to be a Christian, you need to present yourself. It is possible that you do this without being aware of the consequences, but that is true for all the important choices in life. The profession of a Christian is an act of surrender. You continue to act and think as usual, but you have acknowledged that Christ is the lord of your life. That is why it is important that a specific moment arises when you have become prepared inwardly and your choice is openly visible. It is a moment of profession, or declaration.

That many members nowadays, for the above reason, feel the need for a water ritual, even though they were baptized as an infant, is easy to understand. There is no reason why this request should not be honored one way or another.

Roles

You become a member in order to play a role in the drama of the fellowship of Christ. As is often said, the world is the actual stage for your role. We are not called to sit in the church the whole week. "On Sundays she goes to church" as a popular Dutch song has it, "not the other days." It is assumed that your role in life has to be learned somewhere. The church is a training school to teach you a role.

"Role" is also but a word. Paul writes in his letters about *charisma*, gifts of grace. He writes that the Holy Spirit dispenses these gifts as he wishes (1 Cor 12:11). Paul combines this observation with the image of a body and its members. You have a special gift of grace, and with it you take your place in the body, as a hand or foot or eye or ear. Perhaps the metaphor of a role is somewhat flexible. A foot is always a foot, but you need not play the same role all the time.

When Paul speaks about charismatic gifts, he thinks of it as a special gift the Spirit gives to people. In practice this may mean that you make the most of your natural *talents*. A charisma as a gift of grace is often a "sanctification" of a creation gift. For that matter, there are also gifts that seem to have fallen "directly from the sky." Tongue speaking, for example, or the gift of healing. It appears that "what falls from the sky" is rarer than what derives from a person's nature and abilities. Charismata as present in the average church are more like talents. Even then they are gifts of the spirit. He imparts these talents to serve the life of the congregation.

The congregation is the place where you determine what your gift is and to receive it in faith. You can also use it in the circle of your brothers and sisters. There you learn how to play the game with each other. We could just as well begin with our calling in the world, but it is pleasant that there is also a calling that members of the church have toward each other. That is a specific fellowship which sees to it that your calling takes on a concrete form and is not just a matter of pleasant words.

Together we also play a drama. The roles can be adjusted to each other. Gifts can be liturgical, organizational, diaconal, pastoral, catechetical, didactic, or proclamation, and many others. If we as church members are unable to play with each other in a certain piece, not much will become of our service to the world either. For that matter, this game can also be played with just a small group of players. That is good news for a declining membership. That may call for a lesser text or performance. The main thing is a good assignment of roles. Solo appearances require a different theater.

Church Offices

There are roles in the church called offices. Offices have a special significance. They relate the performance which the congregation enacts explicitly to the script of God. Every person and every human community has from time to time an inclination to deviate from God's script. This means especially that the decisive character of the third act forward, the act of Jesus Christ—his birth, his life, and especially his death and resurrection, is in danger of disappearing. What do I have to do after all with such events as happened to someone in about the year thirty? And how can these events have a bearing on my life? Why need we as a community hold on so tightly to the Lord? Surely, there are additional authorities? These are obvious questions. Even if they are not being asked, they are hiding in the background—questions very real to our lives. It is just because these questions are so obvious that we need office-bearers.

Offices are not meant to take over the game from others who do not hold an office. Let each one continue in his role or start to play a role in the congregation. Offices are not meant either to organize everything in a congregation or to see to it that everything goes well. Church offices are therefore intended for the players and the congregation to adhere to their roles. They will ask you as a member of the congregation whether within and outside the congregation you are still playing a Christian role. They ask whether you as a member of the congregation are keeping faith with God's drama, and whether they are prepared to fill the gap between the third and fifth acts. They encourage you to continue to play your role avidly.

A special church office is that of the ministry of the word and sacrament. It is there that the script of God gets laid out, interpreted, and presented. Without this office, the congregation would be no more than a club. Sometimes people talk that way about the church. That may sound practical, but it misses the point. That image of the church as a club suggests that the ultimate leadership is in human hands, and that the goals are defined by the leadership of the club. A congregation is not a club, but the very body of Christ. It is a community that is taken over by Christ. It is not a community which itself already knows which game is to be played and decides so with majority vote. Rather, it is a community that is prepared to work along with God and in interaction with Christ. And, therefore, to keep the focus on these proceedings, there is the special office of the ministry of the Word and sacrament. Through this office we get a continuous production, one in which the theme will not be modified halfway through. This office is, on the one hand, an ugly obstacle to the constant inclination to adapt the play or to let it harden. This office, on the other hand, is a beautiful service, one which binds us with the only narrative which creates real joy and the only piece that contains hope for the future.

This office is transferred with the light gesture of laying on of hands, from the days of the apostles until now. Despite all changes and flexibility, communities remain which still proceed to enact this original script.

The Apocalypse

We are acting in the drama of God, and we are sitting in the fourth act, as was said earlier. The church as theater is not an altogether innocent metaphor. It is not really about producing scripts or giving lectures or speeches. The image of the church as it is described in the New Testament comes through as having more apocalyptic features than harmonious ones.

Paul, the greatest apostle of Christendom, had no illusions over the place he occupied as leader. He writes about the apostles, "For it seems to me God has made us apostles the last act in the show, like men condemned to death in the arena, a spectacle to the whole universe, to angels as well as men" (1 Cor 4:9). By being faithful to Christ, Paul has ended up at the spot where people get hit with hard blows, where he feels as if he has been condemned to death, someone ridiculed by spectators in a Roman theater. The actor in the drama of Christ gets assigned the lowest place in the theater of the state. That is also the theater of being laughed at, and bloodthirstiness. Paul takes it ill of the church of Corinth that they have chosen the position of honor and respect. That position points to the future, but it is not yet here.

Where Christ appears on the stage, the antichrist also gets active. Christ's defenseless willing to self-sacrifice arouses the power of evil. The evil of the antichrist manifests itself not so much in playing devilish tricks, but by building an alternative for the kingdom of Christ. It is a messianic utopia, without sacrifice, without the cross, with happiness for all mankind, under the aura of the true benefactors of mankind, and, therefore, a utopia of flag-waving and parades, with bread and games, and, if necessary, involving tanks and grenades.

The church stands on this battlefield. That is not always perceptible. Europe has experimented with a so-called Constantinian Christendom. After his conversion, Emperor Constantine declared Christianity to be the official, authoritative religion. Europe is the continent in which the process of Christianizing took place. Differences may exist about this proposal, but this one thing is certain: we are living in a period where post-Christianity has come to settle in. In the history of the preceding century, the church has been confronted with the ruthless ideologies of Nazism, communism, and materialistic capitalism. The greatest temptation has been to go along with these ideologies and, thus, to accommodate ourselves to them. Fortunately, there have always been a core of true believers who have resisted these ideologies. The dominant ideologies today are secular, appearing now in the forms of liberalism, socialism, or nationalism. Christian faith is being driven to the margins of private existence. Even some recognition of the significance of the church and faith in public life is gone. That is the stark reality of the church in the Western world.

Church and Christian life should not let itself be rocked to sleep by the spirit of the times. Although the church will be open to all that is good in contemporary culture, willing and ready to heed and strive to attain good for contemporary life and existing solidly alongside the community, it must all the while nevertheless remain faithful to the script which they are performing. Fundamental choices cannot be avoided. One cannot serve God and mammon at the same time. Being faithful to Christ and surrender to him implies a refusal to play in the act of big money. I see it happen that faith in the drama of Christ himself will lead to even clearer choices. Who knows, that may mean the end of the overemphasis on differences in church and Christendom. In retrospect, they have mostly been deluxe matters anyway.

The Bible describes in apocalyptic, vivid colorful images the contest between good and evil. In quieter times, these texts were permitted to sleep under the dust. They can, however, wake up and arouse a church which itself had become too sleepy and stuffy. This is true because the fourth act will not be a sleepy lethargic production but a piece of great tensions and principled alternatives. We don't go through the final days and enter eternity just like that. The last parables in the gospels speak of tension. When the Lord comes, will he find us awake? Or, as Jesus put it, "Keep awake then, for you know neither the day nor the hour when he will come" (Matt 25:13). Walking away is the permanent temptation. It can be offset only by prayer, alertness, and fasting.

5

The Church as Parliament

Church and Politics

TO DESCRIBE THE CHURCH as a parliament asks for some introduction and, therefore, some patience on the part of the reader. With this metaphor we enter the terrain of politics, and I must say something about that. I must also say something about the church as a "political body" before I can address the theme of parliament itself.

To set foot on the turf of the political is beset with danger. Merging church and politics is not desirable for either. The separation of church and state says it well. Whereas politics (the state) is not permitted to encroach on the terrain of the church, the church, on the other hand, is not to encroach on the terrain of politics. In the last instance, the church becomes politicized and loses its true identity.

However true that may be, the church nowadays must overcome its cold water fear of the political domain. When that happens, the church quickly becomes merely an institution for the satisfaction of religious needs. Or, it becomes an educational institution for a highly principled life. Or, it becomes a society for charitable deeds. That is a painful deviation from what the church actually is. And for that reason I choose the metaphor of the church as parliament. And in that setting the Christian community is a parliament.

The Church as a Political Body

The church is a fellowship of people who are not ruled ultimately by earthly regimes. Even less is the church established on the initiatives of citizens. The church is the body of Christ himself. There would be no church if Christ had not risen from the dead, if the Holy Spirit had not been poured out, and if the apostles had not been sent out into the world. The church is a fellowship of people, but this fellowship stands or falls with Jesus Christ and the Holy Spirit. There is but one true head of the church, and that is Jesus Christ. In the world itself and in the communities of this world, there is a new fellowship from those communities who come together in the name of Christ and who listen to Christ.

Believers acknowledge Jesus as Lord. The oldest confession known to us is "Jesus is Lord" (1 Cor 12:3). That was a daring confession. "Lord," after all, is the equivalent of the Greek word *kurios*, a word that the Romans appropriated as *Caesar*. That could initiate a conflict. It is not as if Jesus set himself on the throne of authority. He said that his kingdom is not of this world. In any case Jesus announced that he does not intend to form a political entity in opposition to the authorities of this world. The thrones of the rulers remain in place for the time being, until the day when all earthly rulers will be dismissed and the kingdom of God will be established. Until that time, political arrangements must remain in place. There must be a structure which restrains evil and serves the common good. It must be an arrangement assigned to achieve justice for all, and peace among people.

Truly, the power of this political institution is significantly restricted. In the first place, it is only temporary. The future lies with Jesus, before whom one day all powers will bow. The rich of this world and their authorities will disappear. It is not as a super power that Jesus claims the future; it is rather because he was prepared to bear the cross of the world and to sacrifice himself for the world. The future belongs to the crucified one. In the second place, the power of the temporal authorities is limited in what they can accomplish. They can do something, but not everything. They cannot provide eternal life. Political powers are not saints. They cannot forgive sins, nor can they impart righteousness and sanctification. They do well to avoid pretensions, especially in their pursuit of worldly goods. In the third place, they are limited in their authority itself. They must not infringe on the consciences of their people. The hearts do not belong to those in power.

Holders of power are often tempted to transgress these boundaries. They wish always to extend their sway. They want to rule forever and establish everlasting kingdoms. They wish to be seen as sacred figures and also establish a community. They wish to rule over the consciences and hearts of mankind. They would love to banish freedom of thought, but, surely, at the least, freedom of speech. They become restive when compelled to abide by these restrictions.

There is a group of people who call on the authorities to remain within the boundaries. Those are the ones who believe in Jesus as Lord. They are not a set of revolutionaries who wish to seize power. They are even less a set of folks who view the government with disdain. Usually they are loyal citizens who recognize that government "does not wield the sword in vain" (Rom 13:4). They pay their taxes, they concern themselves for the general well being, and so on. But one thing they will not do: they will not recognize a government which transgresses the boundaries described above. They refuse to do so in the name of God, but also on account of the genuine human community. And, therefore, if they are ever called upon to acknowledge Caesar as a deity, they will refuse to do so. Caesar is no *kurios*—that is, one who thinks too much of himself. There is only one who deserves divine honor, and that is Jesus. The martyrs among the early Christians were prepared to be thrown into the arena to maintain their fidelity to the Lord. Here lies the potential cause of conflict that will exist between the rulers of the world and of the church.

Thinking of the church as a political body, therefore, does not mean that the church wishes to have power. When that occurs, the church has become "worldly" and denies Christ. He refused the offer to obtain political power. The church should do the same. What the church should strive to be is a community in which Jesus has the authority. That is what Jesus desired—erecting a community consisting of men who have been rescued and who live together as brothers and sisters. Jesus did not welcome loose imitators, but a fellowship of true believers. He has promised to be present wherever two or three are gathered in his name.

On the other hand, Jesus' authority is seen especially in the giving of the people to the Lord and in living as a new community. So it is true indeed that Jesus proclaimed the kingdom, and that then the church arrived—the church, that is, as a community of brothers and sisters, united in the name of Jesus. Now we are approaching the metaphor of the church as parliament. That is to say, this metaphor refers to the church as a fellowship under the lordship of Jesus Christ. When Christ rules and is in charge, it does not happen in an authoritative manner. Paul writes, "Now the Lord of whom this passage speaks is the Spirit; and where the Spirit of the Lord is, there is liberty" (2 Cor 3:17). God is not served by slaves, but by children. It is in that context that the metaphor of parliament is relevant. We need, therefore, first to say a few words about a parliament.

The Parliament

A parliament exists for the proper functioning of a mature democracy. Free elections are often seen as the greatest achievement of democracy. It is true that democracy cannot exist without the input of its citizens. That involvement can develop to the point where the citizens choose their own rulers. That does not occur here in the Netherlands. The people vote for a party, and a government is subsequently formed. When necessary, a specialized cabinet is formed in which people take their seat on the grounds of their expertise rather than on their political stance. The core of democracy lies not so much in the practice of citizens choosing their representatives directly, but that the rulers are accountable to the people. That is what happens in a representative parliament.

The institution of parliament is older than free elections. That is why the quality of a parliament says more about the quality of a democracy than about the question of whether representatives are chosen directly by the people. In a parliament the government has to put up with the criticism of people's representatives. Deliberations in parliament are intended to generate laws which will serve the common good. That is always the goal of politics—to give leadership in a way that serves and promotes the common good. That raises the question of what constitutes the common good and human society.

The word *parliament* derives from the French world *parler*, to speak. In a true democracy there is government through the medium of speech. Government is not the product of brutish power plays, but is carried on through conversation, through dialogue, through deliberations about what is good and just. A tyrant forces his will through strategies he imposes by the power of weapons. A democratic government governs by presenting arguments and in a storm-free atmosphere.

How Freedom Encourages Boldness

We return now to the community of Christ. Christ rules there, but not without a parliament. The entire congregation is a parliament. It is, in fact, a community which exists of equal people. The differences are overcome in Christ. They exist, to be sure, but they are not decisive. Whether you are man or woman, poor or rich, white or colored, heterosexual or homosexual—let all that be, but these differences are not decisive. Far more important is being accepted by Jesus and, therefore, becoming one through him (Gal 3:28). That implies that in the congregation everybody is counted as equal and entitled to participate.

A word that looms large in the New Testament is the word *parrhesia*, boldness in conversation. That means that everybody is allowed to speak. Jesus taught his disciples to address God as Father. "The spirit you have received is not a spirit of slavery, leading you back into a life of fear, but a Spirit of adoption enabling us to say "Abba! Father!" (Rom 8:15). *Parrhesia* refers also to the freedom to speak to people in the name of God. It is confidence to speak about anything with anyone which involves the well-being of the fellowship. "Be subject to one another out of reverence for Christ," writes the apostle (Eph 5:21). Authority is not a hierarchically structured system in which one speaks and another listens and obeys. Every member of the congregation has his own authority. It is the authority with which the Holy Spirit endows him. On that basis, he speaks as he himself is spoken to by another. Perhaps that is the apex of freedom, to voluntarily accept the authority of another in acknowledging that the other really has something to say.

The congregation is a parliament. There one may feel free to speak. In public worship we need a certain order, but Paul is not niggardly about allowing people inspired by the Holy Spirit to speak out. "Let the gospel of Christ dwell among you in all its richness; teach and instruct one another with all the wisdom it gives you. With psalms and hymns and spiritual songs, sing from the heart in gratitude to God" are the words with which Paul instructs us (Col 3:16). The congregation is the space where the free word flourishes, since the Word, through the Spirit, has been given to everyone. The Spirit is the true democrat, through whom "your sons and daughters shall prophesy . . . and also your servants and handmaidens" (Acts 2:17, 18).

Obviously, the gift of leadership has also been given to the Christian congregation. It is part of every community. From the very beginning of the church there were apostles, elders, and overseers. I wrote earlier about church offices. But the purpose of these leaders is not to rule over the people. True leadership points to Christ as the true head. The key word in the church is not ruling, but service. "Whoever wants to be great must be your servant" (Mark 10:43). Such leadership is accountable. Leadership is not intended to subject people into yourself (the leader), but to teach people with Christ, and encourage them to stay with Christ. He who preaches "another gospel" is, according to Paul, even condemned (Gal 1:8). And Paul includes himself. The least brother or sister in the congregation has the right to challenge the leadership about this. It is the Spirit itself which gives the courage to do so. Paul wrote his letter to the entire congregation and, thus, makes the whole congregation articulate. He wishes with his letters to arouse the "faith of the congregation" so that the members will not be led astray from the gospel by leaders. Opposing the power of such leaders, he offered the power of the word from an apostle and the free deliberations of the congregation. Let there be no leader without a parliament. Let there be no church offices without articulate fellow members.

Conversation about the Good Life

The quality of a parliament is not only about the quality of the leadership. It is mainly about the question of how the Spirit of Christ pervades the life of the believers and the life of the congregation. In the congregation, the subject of conversation is God—about life with God, about the life of the fellowship, about life in the world. How good it is that there is such a place where this conversation can be conducted. A church is not merely a building with benches where you sit quietly in order to hear some narrative or other and then silently return home. The presence of benches is not a problem; nevertheless, a congregation is also a circle. In that way you as an individual can grow. You may be meaningful to another person, and another person may be meaningful for you. In this parliament the conversation is all about the general well-being of the congregation.

All this is, of course, an altogether different parliament from the one that convenes in The Hague. In this parliament, for example, the emphasis is not on laws. Nor does it concern itself exclusively with the management of the congregation. It is concerned, rather, with life through the Spirit and life in Christ. The purpose is to bring the impact of Christ on our lives. That does not come to us in a blinding lightning flash from above. That occurs through encouragement, coaching, correction, meditation, and prayer. That is how each person builds the other up to form an authentic fellowship.

Sometimes there is a weighing of the pros and cons. This is to "approve of things that really matter" (Phil 1:10). That requires a fine sensitivity, and that does not happen without an openness that permits mutual conversation and reflection. Sometimes the subject requires weighty deliberation.

Detached from this parliament, you as a Christian swim all by yourself in the pond of this world. Without this parliament, the authority of Christ will not have much chance. You miss the give and take of conversation. You cook in your own stew, and that is thin gruel. You quickly grow eccentric. Your energy dries up, your sensitivities become blunted, you become a one-man oracle, you become arrogant. To be sure, my style of life is my own, but that can develop only in openness and receptivity toward your brothers and sister, and especially to what the Holy Spirit may be wishing to communicate in this context. On the other hand, you also have things to say. Why should you keep your insights and wisdom to yourself?

In this setting the church becomes a training ground for life as a follower of Jesus. It is the place where moral deliberation takes place. In this way, the gospel helps us to see through the poverty of the false gods of the day. It helps above all for one to lead a life which knows about the Creator, who knows that life is a gift, and who understands the art of extending love to God and neighbor. There is talking in this parliament. The spirit of Christ moves among people when they converse with each other. In this way God's purpose with life and our life together comes into being. We can hardly afford, therefore, to ignore such a parliament.

Intercession as Mutual Conversation

Parrhesia, a boldness of spirit, speaks of freedom. That point, as said earlier, points us in the first place to God. God is highly approachable, and it is not obligatory for us to kneel before a mute mystery in abject silence. The children of God speak boldly with the Eternal one. This permits an intimate conversation between God and every person, a conversation that is not subject to the judgment of others. This pertains as well to the prayers of the congregation to God. People pray together. That prayer makes clear the truth that the congregation is a parliament. The congregation thinks along with God. God is the highest authority and the highest power, and the congregation is given to Christ as his body. He does not, however, rule like a tyrant. The congregation is a parliament and has the right to speak. This occurs especially in the prayer. "God rules the world through the prayers of his children."[1]

The intercessory prayer should not be regarded as a wish list of suggested topics laid before God. In intercessions, people, nations, groups are brought before God. Believers are involved in and think about what is happening and talk to God. God rules, but he gives heed to the petitions people present to him. Whenever the rule of God is regarded as a mechanical unwinding of formal petitions, it becomes "For you, but without you." It is a caricature of the image of God which the Bible conveys.

We see that as we look to Jesus. Through him God brings in the kingdom of God. But the way in which Jesus related to people was not by way of commands. A Gentile woman approached Jesus with the urgent plea that he liberate her daughter from an evil spirit. Jesus first put her off with the words, "It is not right to take the children's bread and throw it to the dogs." The woman got up enough courage to say, "Sir, even the dogs under the table eat the children's scraps." That reply prompted Jesus to reply, "For saying that, Go, and you will find the demon has left you daughter" (Mark 7:24–30).

Intercessory prayer is prayer for yourself and for others. It is often the case that we represent others. Perhaps the others are unable to pray. The church, therefore, does that for them. Even if they are able, a community of believers takes it upon itself to represent others. Shouldn't there be a parliament that represents humanity before God? It is a high honor to represent another. Indeed, is there a greater honor for a person than to represent someone else before God? And that not only for "your own people," but for others? Through the Spirit the church opens wide its eyes and arms.

The Art of Agreement

The children of God speak boldly with God. That conversation concerns their own life, that of others, and that of the world. Sometimes God's children challenge God. They cannot understand what has occurred. They don't agree with it. They dare to complain. Sometimes complaints turn into accusation. The book of Job is a good example. He rebels against his bitter fate. And Job does not stand alone. The Bible tells us clearly not to swallow, nor cringe. The parliament does not necessarily follow the highest authority. There is freedom and boldness to ask why and why not.

1. Gunning, "Voorbede," 31.

And yet something else can happen. You can come to agree with God. That is probably the highest level attainable. One can say Yea and Amen to this, both as an individual believer and as a believing community. This parliament can even praise and glorify God. At least it can say Amen. That is not a superficial Amen. It is not a cheap Amen. Nevertheless, it rings true. Yea and Amen is said in the congregation. God receives praise for his works. The congregation finally agrees with how God rules. It is especially one with God because he reigns with Jesus. It especially agrees with a God who rules through the cross, the one who raises people from the dead, the one who shows concern for the poor. It is at one even though it does not have a complete knowledge of all things. It trusts the leading of God, even though questions remain. God, after all, is good, and life in this world remains in good hands. A church service is a conversation in which the last word is Amen. God has convinced us again. We do not stick to reservations and objections. The kingdom of Christ has again been demonstrated. We do not live in perpetual uneasiness, and even less as a perennial complainer. It is wholesome to be freed from all of these. The final chord, therefore, is a hymn of praise, and the final word is Amen. Nothing more need be said. Parliament is dismissed. We have been sent out, and we can return to our homes.

A Free Word for Our Communal Life

In a true democracy the authorities listen to voices from the public domain. This occurs, obviously, through the parliament, but no limits can be imposed. All voices are welcome, not only the voices of those whose official position it is to speak. The authorities themselves participate in a broad civic debate over various cases. A democracy invites a parliament and, necessarily, others as well to speak out for the *common good*. By so doing, it also hears the voice of the church. That lies ready to hand, given the obvious fact that the proclamation of the church has been one of the factors which has made Europe what it is. It is a bad sign whenever a government is ominously prompted to take the church seriously because of the so-called separation of church and state. Without minimizing a healthy separation of church and state, a government does wise when it listens to "prophecy"— voices which speak of moral principles based on inspired writings which do not coincide with the prevailing opinion of the official government culture. The church is not a shadow parliament for the government and must not see itself in that light. In this fellowship you find an open attitude and loyalty toward the political arena. Where is there a fellowship in our life together which is so loyal in this respect, that it prays for, and wishes God's blessings on her?

Naturally, the church has opinions about the political business of this world. Where necessary, it will also have something to say about political cases. In doing so we need to take the proper boundaries into consideration. The church must not continuously busy itself with specific application of the laws and even less must it make a shadow budget for the kingdom of the Netherlands. But when it concerns human dignity (and is that not the case all the time?) it should make its voice heard. Even without making official declarations, she will raise her voice. The quality of our common good is a good thing but under constant challenge. A one-sided emphasis on economic growth at the cost of humanity and the earth is a form of tyranny which needs to be challenged. Without being argumentative, we can, in God's name, make the case that a flourishing life and community is a matter that deserves to be dealt with.

By the way, I intend to mean by the word "church" not only the leadership of national churches, or churches international, or churches with a similar faith profession. The church is in the first place the local congregation. "The church" are the members of such a local church in their life with each other and in their relationship with others. Prophetic voices are not specifically declarations but arise from living as a Christian community and with the intent of being a blessing to others.

6

The Church as Temple

CHURCH AND TEMPLE ARE realities that are near to each other. Some church buildings are even called temples. They are not, however, identical. The autonomous temple in the Bible, the center of worship, was destroyed long ago. The first temple was abandoned when the tribe of Judah was deported to Babylon. The second temple was destroyed by the Romans in AD 70. Already before this time, Christendom had likely broken with that temple. The sacrificial rituals were no longer necessary, now that the sacrifice of Christ had been fulfilled. It was rather the liturgy of the Jewish synagogue which served as the model of worship for the early Christians. Still, the memory of the temple persisted. An institution which has had an important place for centuries and governed a whole culture in its jurisdiction is still strong enough to serve as a *trigger* for the memory. And it can shed light on what a church is and what happens in a church.

I intend, thus, to call attention to three points of comparison. In the first place, the appearance of God, spatially, in a building. Secondly, the worship of God as the highest deed man can perform. Thirdly, the being together as believers in the divine worship. The temple creates a liturgical community.

The Temple as a Place Where We Appear before God

The temple is above all the place where one appears before God with songs of praise and a thankful heart. To appear before God: that sounds stately and ceremonious, but without such expressions, life becomes exceedingly simplistic. The temple was situated on Mt. Zion, and the pilgrims marched up to it, from near and far, to enter their place of worship. The song puts it this way:

> Send out your light and your truth,
> to be my guide.
> Let them lead me to your holy hill,
> To your dwelling place. (Ps 43:3)

From their routine lives, the pilgrims made the journey to the mountain of God. From your own place you trek to the residence of God, over there, over the horizon, in order to appear before God. God is there. There you appear before his very face.

We still have a sense of this experience. One of the reasons why a pilgrimage is so appealing lies right here. It is a real experience, one fraught with deep emotion, to arrive at the sanctuary after a long stretch of weeks or even months. It makes a great difference whether you arrive at the sanctuary after a long ascent or via an elevator. It is not the same if you arrive somewhere after many days by foot or by plane. To worship God requires a place, a building, but also a way to get to that place. The attraction of a church building lies right here. Therefore, it is best, if possible, to walk to the church.

To be sure, one can meet God anywhere. For that, as Jesus said, we need to worship him "in Spirit and in truth" (John 4:24). Therefore, you are not obliged to go to Jerusalem. From an altogether different angle, the word "place" in modern times, our digital era, becomes severely relativized. The digital culture links us with wherever we want to be. What meaning can there still be to a geographical place?

But that can lead to dehumanization. We are people of time and place. We are that as well in our worship of God. To forego a time and a place for worship makes our lives unbearable. The church building relates our worship of God to a specific space set apart for that purpose. The building acquires, especially over the course of years, a sense of sacredness.

All this calls for prudence when it comes to monumental church buildings. They were and are places of divine worship, and that in some sense has turned the stones into something sacred. Here the people of God used to worship, and here they come still. Also, if the buildings stand empty and are no longer used for worship, we can still associate it with prayer and worship, provided that we have an intuition for this. Even if such a place were to turn into a ruin, somewhere, in the middle of nowhere, it can happen that a passerby might experience an irresistible longing to kneel.

Even ugly church buildings, through use, can become sanctified. The smell, the cross on the wall, a pulpit, the semi-darkness, the organ—all of these can arouse memories which can awaken a new occasion for worship.

Perhaps it is necessary for me to say all this more boldly: In order to meet God in our society, you need above all to get out of your own house. It is too difficult to meet God in houses. The idea that worship is a private matter, "behind the front door," is untenable. To meet God you must leave the front door behind you in order to get outdoors and to a place of public worship. People as private human beings no longer come to God. For a long time already, the gods of this world have taken over the private world. No double pane of glass exists to oppose them. The popular dialogue between public and private is, on closer look, not as exciting as it might at first appear. The world penetrates our lives more than we think. There is but one way of escape: the church building, whatever it may look like. It can even be a living room which has been arranged and set aside as church space for a worship service at home. How good that there is a house dedicated to God. It is there we appear before God. To be sure, God is everywhere. But a God who is everywhere is, eventually, nowhere.

The Temple as the Place Where God Manifests Himself

"Appearing before God" is one of the loveliest expressions among phrases which enrich our language. Implied in it is the belief that God also goes to church. Obviously, no wrapping can capture him, and no building can hold him. God is everywhere, and, thus, we can meet him anywhere, but his face is here, and now. His divinity pervades endless rooms, but his *eyes* rest on this place and his *ears* are tuned to this time. Such was the intuition of ancient Israel.

Meanwhile, from the single establishment of the temple, an enormous number of temples have been reproduced and have become a staggering plurality. In place of one temple, we have many church buildings. God is faithful in his attendance at church, far more faithful than we realize. That may seem like an insult, for how can the eternal, infinite God now become associated with a church building? Doesn't this reduce God to the level of a small-minded spirit? The danger is real. A church building can also turn into an empty, drafty skeleton. Every claim made on God by a church community is one too many. But our broad-mindedness is not always a safe guide when we talk about God. God in his freedom has also chosen to be a God of times and places. The likelihood of his appearance is not just anywhere and everywhere. As people assemble in a church building on the day of the resurrection, it is done in awareness and belief, as the hymn has it:

> God is here; he is here in our midst.
> Let us worship him, from the depths, prostrate,
> God is among us, let everything be silent,
> And let all that we are bow down to him.
> (*Liedboek voor de kerken*, 323:1)

The Temple as a Place to Praise and to Offer Thanks

The temple is the place where people come together to appear before God and worship him. Not that this is useful, or advantageous in some way, but because planted deep into our hearts is the inclination to go beyond ourselves in order to praise and offer thanks. From a strictly economic perspective, in terms of energy management, it looks like a waste of energy that is better used for something else. Fortunately, we are, human beings, not machines, who regularly escape the bond of what is useful. We dance, we leap, we dream and fantasize; we reach for the land beyond the horizon. Life breathes truly only in a land with open horizons.

The urge to worship is the ultimate expression of this outlook. The one who reveres God really steps out from the closed circuit of investments and profits. The authentic life is never a closed circuit. It is transcendent. "L'homme passe infiment l'homme" (Man infinitely transcends man).[1] We do not mean transcending in the sense of being a hybrid, Übermensch (Nietzsche), a creature who finally loses his humanity, but, rather, in the direction of God. Through thanksgiving, worship, and praise, we leave the narrow room of ourselves and enter the space of God. The church is the place where the deep-seated desires of the heart receive their voice. It is the sound room which echoes the idea of dependence and transcendence. It is the open place in an existence directed toward transcendence and which finds its rest in God, who is eternal and infinite.

1. Pascal, *Pensées*, Fragment 131.

This is true, though it cannot be proven. Worship and praise can, indeed, be seen as hand-clapping before an empty heaven. I would say: Even that would be worth the trouble. Better the man who claps and sings than the man who only creeps like a busy ant over the earth. Better the cricket than the ant. Better the dancer on the shore of a silent sea than the commoner seated on the shore.

But I believe that praise and thanksgiving are something else than dancing on an empty shore before a silent sea. Praise and thanksgiving are responses to a word; they are the radiation of man as a response to the outpouring of God. God generously radiates goodness and truth. We are surrounded by this goodness. God lets us see that goodness every morning when he lets the sun rise on the evil and the good (Matt 5:45). Moreover, God's goodness takes on bodily form, and his truth becomes tangible. Belief and praise exist because these things can be heard. It is a special revelation. God is a giving God who from early on has chosen to give himself to man.

And for this reason, there is also a response to this revelation. All this leaping and praise and prayer and thanks are reflective responses to grace and truth. Gifts abundant call for surrender, love calls for worship, goodness calls for thankfulness. There is a time and a place where this is done consciously. Not just incidentally, but as intentional acts. Only in this way can traffic occur between earth and heaven; only in this way can human life unfold authentically. Much of our lives happen routinely and unconsciously—also in our relationship to God. But what is more beautiful than choosing to stand in prayer and song, and, audibly and visibly, to present ourselves before the face of the Creator?

Liturgy

Thanksgiving and praise are activities that occur in the temple. They are communal acts which require reciprocal acts. Praise and thanksgiving occur with voice and instrument, and with solos and choirs, and that requires some structure. This all creates musical organization, a culture of song, a liturgy. These activities become widely distributed and developed, over time, into a great variety. People make their way in the world lonely and scattered, but they will always unite in an *ensemble* and together sing God's praise.

Worship occurs spontaneously, but where it acquires a communal expression, a liturgical order comes into being. Liturgical regulations exist that arose in the tradition of a congregation. They "streamline" the worship service. To be sure, each individual must worship God in his own way, but a church also has a kind of acquired liturgical order of worship, a deliberative manner of worship. It is pleasant when people spontaneously dance and sing, but it is no less gratifying to learn dance steps in the study and to learn a hymn. That applies also in divine worship. Thus, no longer do we need to worship God in an *ad hoc* manner. Worship is a holy affair, and so there has been in the tradition much reflection about liturgy and liturgical order. It can be of much help for that resource to be made a part of this order. It elevates you as a human being to a higher level.

Naturally, every good thing can be corrupted, or a part become an end in itself. That danger arises whenever a liturgy becomes a rigid order of worship, in which adhering to and protecting the order has a way of becoming the most important. That occurs whenever the praise is the completion of a series of required acts performed without a spark of joy. A bystander would be unable to guess that here the creature shines before the face of his Creator. The impression that it leaves is probably that these difficult "songs of the club" had been sung because this is the way things have to be.

I do not intend to say by this that a liturgy should consist of odds and ends and has to be popular. There may be different forms of liturgy that require introduction. Songs of praise can contain highly developed forms which may be strange to those not familiar with them. There are also popular forms which, when they reach the ears of the elite, sound like unsophisticated jingles. There is high and low liturgy, there is liturgy for regular services and liturgy for festivals, liturgy with a fixed tune and whole notes, and liturgy which threatens to set the roof of the building ablaze. All is well, just so long as it becomes clear that in one way or another liturgy is the highest level of creaturely activity that exists. If that cannot be guessed even from nearby, something is really wrong.

The Temple as the Center of a Congregation

The temple at Jerusalem constituted the center of the people's lives in ancient Israel. The temple, even more than the palace, was the site around which the people assembled. That is no different from most cultures. The following citation expresses that forcibly:

> There is no life that is not in community
> And no community not lived in praise of God.
> (T. S. Eliot, "Choruses from The Rock")

That is, there is no community which is not rooted in praise of God. The Western world has diverged from this trend. No longer are most of the fellowships in the West liturgical fellowships. The Dutch nation is no longer a liturgical fellowship. The palace rather than the temple is the cohering force. Where the church declines, other centers will appear, especially the shopping marts. People will flock there on Sunday as well, hungering and thirsting after the things of this world, either bored or content. And so life glides by, the precious days of their years. Meanwhile, the soul is at its last gasp. The people will worship something because they are incurably religious, but it is the lesser gods of the day which for a moment unite people, though it does not elevate them. The cult is gone, what remains? Perhaps the culture consists of bread and games; perhaps it is a culture of concert halls and museums. All of this is more or less pleasant and good, but they do not truly bring people together, and they do not really promote their true well-being.

To look longingly to the past when all this was different is nostalgia. We live in a secular world in which each person seeks salvation in his own way or is not at all interested in getting saved. Civic fellowship and faith-based fellowship are not identical. Still, there are faith communities in the midst of civic organizations. Perhaps they are the corks that secretly keep a community afloat more than one is aware of.

The Congregation

Church as temple points to worship as the deed of a *community*. That congregation may consist only of a pair of older women, to which a janitor and an organist may be added, but numbers are not decisive in the realm of praising God. In an extreme case, an individual may himself be the community and keep up the praise. But, normally, two or three are seen as the lower limit.

On the other hand, it is the song of praise that forms a community. Nothing binds people together more than that. That becomes palpable in some degree at festivals and in stadiums. Music and song blend together. But usually such communal events are of short duration. In a fellowship of believers, the collective worship of God is what binds the people together, and, since God is eternal, it gives permanence to this fellowship.

Obviously, a community of believers is more than a liturgical community. There is more than singing. There is also faith, belief. And there are deeds. Besides, you must be clear about which God it is you worship.

Communal worship is not separate from *which* God is worshipped and offered thanks. You thank God for who he is and what he does. You must have a notion about that. So it is understandable that a community is firmly linked together by the same faith, and that this faith is professed in a common confession. Together we praise the same God. Similarly, statements of faith are found in the churches, and it is well that it is so. You worship God also with your mind.

But even confessions can lead their own lives. A community of faith shares the faith, but it lives from a collective worship of God. It is a critical sign whenever the confession comes separated from worship. The church then becomes a theological fraternity instead of a worshipping assembly. That leads often to endless debates, to hot heads and cold hearts, with the consequent break in the fellowship which frequently leads to further divisions. Who knows how many people have been turned off from church by such polarization?

The same must be said about the concept of *ethos*. More is required than worshipping God. There is life with each other, life with others. A congregation becomes united through a comprehensive ethos. Detached from this ethos, worship of God becomes false. How can you love God and offer him thanks when you despise or hate your neighbor? The prophets condemned such attitudes in flaming words. The God who is worshipped is the God who shows compassion for all and whose eyes are especially on the young and the unimportant of the world.

On the other hand, the ethos must not become detached from the liturgy. When that happens, the church becomes a non-government organization, a do-good institution, or a philanthropic establishment. Sooner or later such become joyless and fanatic affairs. Worship and ethos belong together, and it is the worship of God which bears us up and keeps alive the care of the neighbor.

PART 4

The Realities

1

Introduction

A Thoughtful Afterword

THIS LAST PART CAN be regarded as a bonus. It has to do with reality. Whoever does not attach much importance to it or, upon a description of it does not come across anything of interest, is better off to close this book and do whatever he or she thinks is proper with what has gone before. One who, on the other hand, is not so easily toppled over and who can handle a more contemplative section is welcome to read on. I write it as a thoughtful conclusion, an afterthought. Until now we have been concerned with the relationship between earth and heaven. The heaven, that is, God, who manifests himself to man. The earth, that is man, who believes in God. The interplay between the two is many faceted and multivoiced. It is a serious drama, and all who participate in it do so with gusto. The church belongs in that drama. It is the stage on which the play gets enacted. Without this stage and the interaction on it, not much of importance can be said about this drama. It is played out under the title "Abundance and Response"—over-flowing kindness from God's side and response from man's side. We could have concluded the book on this note.

But I wish to go further. I wish to open up a broader perspective and consider questions about Reality. The book up to this point could be considered as a pleasant narrative for those who will believe it—a pious fiction, not false, but a fiction, a human portrayal, a dream above the abyss, misty cobwebs in the autumn, upon which the sun shines only to disappear. Belief in God is then a pleasant narrative which shields the eyes from hard realities, intended for people who are not tough enough to face this reality. That is what prompts me to say something about that reality.

I do this not in order to further prove the foregoing. Apart from faith and a faith community, God cannot be proved. Nor do I claim that this reality is obvious. Generally speaking, our nature is such that we always view reality through human eyes. We all wear glasses. Those glasses are our mind, our attitude, our heart, our way of living, and how we view life. There are glasses that make reality flat and small. There are also glasses that give us a broader outlook on life. Faith could be called a pair of 3D glasses through which we see reality as three dimensional. Of course, in that case, a basic assumption is the belief that reality is (at least) three dimensional. The spectacles of faith, it turns out, are the ones that do the greatest justice to reality. Not every take on reality fulfills these conditions. There are weaker and richer holds on it. I am about to describe an understanding of reality which is most compatible with the three-dimensional spectacles of faith.

This concept is based on viewing reality as manifestations of truth, goodness, and beauty. They are not arbitrary terms. They go back to at least the times of Plato and Aristotle. But they keep returning, and even today they are often found useful. They correspond very well with a Christian view of reality. These terms purport to examine reality at its deepest levels. Since the reality of our daily life is based on truth, goodness, and beauty, we need to give them some attention. We could, of course, instead of speaking about truth, goodness, and the beautiful, also talk about *the* truth, *the* goodness, and *the* beautiful. Or, to be even more specific, we could speak about *this* truth, *this* goodness, *this* beauty. Indeed, we could just as well speak about *these* truths, *these* good things, *these* beauties. But to avoid the necessity of resorting to all these words every time, I shall, for the sake of brevity, use the words *truth, goodness*, and *beauty*.

As already said, in practice these terms coexist with a Christian world view. On the other hand, these terms enable us to put into words and explain a Christian world view and practice. That Christian narrative is not a sort of abracadabra. It does not exist apart from normal inquiries of people. That narrative has to do with the ultimate questions of life with which philosophers, thinkers, and poets have busied themselves. A faith that moves away from this inquiry not only makes it too easy for itself but also escapes into a world all its own, a world unapproachable for others. And that problem must be faced. That is why this chapter is both useful and necessary.

God as the Source

Truth, goodness, and beauty lie in the domain of reality because, so I believe, God is their creator. They also come from God. God is their source. One could take this a step further and say that God is himself truth, goodness, and beauty, and that reality is a reflection, an image, of him. God is the true, the good, and the beautiful. There would be no truth, goodness, or beauty if God did not exist.

It is true that people could be hospitable to truth, goodness, and beauty without believing in God. The fact is that Reality happens to speak this language, and there is no one who can completely escape it. You would have to deny your very self should you attempt to shut yourself off entirely from truth, goodness, and beauty. Every breath we take is a witness to this trilogy and the basis for every act we perform. It is plain to see that life would be impossible in a world which does not confront us with truth, goodness, and beauty. That would be nothing less than a hell on earth. This is the actual world in which all human beings meet each other, believers and unbelievers alike.

Still, not every philosophy leaves room for truth, goodness, and beauty. Nihilism, for example (the outcome of a very critical philosophy), acknowledges very little of these realities. In practice, there is no living with nihilism. How can that be? What seems obvious is that faith equips you with an increased openness to truth, goodness, and beauty. Through the spectacles of faith, the believer sees reality as connected with God. Since you know the source of truth, goodness, and beauty, you have a keener eye to see these in reality. Moreover, now that you have arrived at this point, you are required to give an answer. You must do so in order to live in the truth, through goodness and beauty. You must do so as an act of surrender.

No Invention, but Discovery

The terms *truth*, *goodness*, and *beauty* have a long tradition. That gives them credibility as descriptions of reality. Consequently, they are not to be viewed as human inventions, as if they have sprung out of the human brain. On the contrary, they are to be viewed as emotional and spiritual discoveries. We find reality, and it reveals itself to us as truth, goodness, and beauty. Reality is, thus, not a gray lump, an amorphous composition of arbitrary, catch-all ingredients, a flat pancake without meaning. Reality is even less a pot of clay on which we arbitrarily impose our own forms—forms which we can bake into hard shapes in order to make living possible—though they still remain arbitrary forms.

On the contrary, Reality itself exists as truth, goodness, and beauty. Reality itself speaks the language of truth, goodness, and beauty. That is an abundant overflow of reality. It comes to us as a three-part waterfall. It does that because of who God is. God is the reality between, and in, reality. God fashioned this world and the people in it in order to manifest something of himself. God is himself like a waterfall from which the threesome of truth, goodness, and beauty flow. The world is an expression of all that. Reality, therefore, comes to us and over us in the three branches of truth, goodness, and beauty.

Man as Part of Reality and as Recipient

Man is the being who is the receiver of all this. He is the privileged being who may listen to the reality as truth, goodness, and beauty. He is himself a segment of reality and, thus, also subordinate to truth, goodness, and beauty. A child that is born is true, good, and beautiful. A human face is that as well, by virtue of the fact man has an inalienable dignity. That we as people live together is also obvious. We do not find that out by ourselves; it is a given. That is how life comes to us. But man is not only an aspect of all this; he is also a beneficiary of it. He has the privilege of living in the light of truth, goodness, and beauty. He can see that light, take it to heart, and live accordingly. Unless the man does this—comes to terms with truth, goodness, and beauty—there will not be much to say about them.

Idealism?

Before I go on with some reflections on each of the three verities, permit me two observations. In the first place, is this really a live issue, this concern about truth, goodness, and beauty, or is it so much busy talk? Does our experience correspond to the realities by which we live? It sounds rather idealistic to talk about truth, goodness, and beauty. What do you gain from it as you deal with the rough and tumble of daily life? Or, putting it even stronger, does it ring true? Falsehood dominates, and during your lifetime you can hardly know whether you can believe members of your own family. And goodness? What is so good about a reality in which thousands of people get swept away by a tsunami? And beauty? As if life is a picture gallery. The world is gray and drab, and there is precious little beauty in a run-down district.

Anyone can add his variations to this list of questions. Looked at by itself, what is the point of this story? That we say farewell to this threesome? That the true, the good, and the beautiful must be delivered into the dumpster of discarded philosophies? That no longer must we call a lie a lie, since, without truth, a lie has no meaning? That the consolation of the kindly hand is reduced to the cosmetic gesture of treating tears by wiping up the blood with a cloth? Is that wondrous light in a baby's face, or the kindly look on the face of a gray-haired old man, real? Or not? Indeed, the sober language of Christian belief reports that we live in a fallen world. But we have ears to capture the secret that this world is scheduled for full truth, total good, and unblemished beauty. There is a *Paradise Lost*, but there is also a *Paradise Regained*. That will become evident.

Man as an Interruption

The second point, a note about man. No one can detach himself radically from truth, goodness, and beauty. The life of mankind is based on these verities. At the same time, man is an enigmatic being. He can close his mind to the deeper dimensions of reality. He can reduce his life to a flat pancake. He can define truth, goodness, and beauty as nonsense. He can oppose them in cross-grained fashion. He can live deceitfully, in anger, and in ugliness. None of this is possible with an animal. An animal has no awareness of truth, goodness, and beauty. Thus, it cannot oppose them either. An animal cannot lie; a human being can. A man can be immoral; an animal, not really. Truth, goodness, and beauty do exist.

No one can alter these givens. God has created reality and has expressed himself through it. The birth of each person testifies to that fact. At the same time, truth, goodness and beauty require a choice. You can deny this—to the point of committing suicide, because you undermine your own existence by doing that. Still, it can be done. Truth, goodness, and beauty thrive in the air of freedom. Freely they come to men; freely they want to be admitted and accepted. They knock on the door, rap against the window, finger the wall, and request admittance. They can be refused. According to the sober language of the Christian faith, the latter is far too often the case. Mankind is showing truth, goodness, and beauty the door.

It is questionable whether all of this has been done with full awareness. You would probably have to be a devil to do that. But even though it happens more or less as blind deeds, it happens often enough. The actual question, therefore, is this: How can we restore truth, goodness, and beauty? This form of the question is the only one that can do justice to the reality of our blemished existence.

In the next chapter I will describe these three fundamental categories separately. Although the terms may be abstract categories, I shall try to connect them to the concrete experiences of people.

2

Truth

Three Escape Routes

PILATE FOREVER ASKS THE question What is Truth? He said that in response to Jesus' comment, "My task is to bear witness to the truth. For this
I was born; for this I came into the world, and all who are not deaf to truth
will listen to my voice" (John 18:37). Pilate at that moment played the role
of a skeptic. A skeptical philosopher does not say there is no truth; neither
does he say there is truth. He holds a middle position. This was an easy way
out for Pilate. He now could wash his hands and plead innocence. With
Jesus' claim to be the truth, he now had only one person to deal with. In his
situation, truth was difficult to come by. He understood deep down that the
truth Jesus represented had some currency in the world, and that it would
have consequences for himself. Thus, Pilate was evasive in his confrontation with Jesus when he asked, What is Truth? The reader of John's gospel
is made to think that Pilate was not altogether honest, perhaps not at all
honest. In the face of the truth, there cannot be a neutral position. Better
said, you cannot always take a neutral position. In some situations that may
work well. In some situations it is a relief. As opposed to those who always
insist on precision, or seek judgments with perfect clarity, a modicum of
skepticism is a respite. In many cases, a relaxed position is the way of wisdom. What do we really know? We are but people who are very limited in
our vision. And, yet, this cannot always be right. It is in the nature of man to

show one's colors. We do that in order to affirm what truth is, and to accept the consequences that give our own lives coherence. Pilate's decision may have been a respectable one, but it was, ultimately, faint-hearted.

Another way of escape is open to us. We hear it in the saying, "That is your truth, this is mine." We all, then, have our own truth, and we open ourselves to endless repetition. Truth as "my truth" assures me that my truth has equal standing, and I do not have to bear responsibility for it. I can at least playfully acknowledge that others have a right to their truth. Each one has his own truth, and now if we can only keep from walking on each other's feet, we should get along well.

It is true, of course, that we live with a variety of truths. As long as humanity proceeds on its pilgrim path, it will remain so. But there remains a problem. How can we explain that some truths are nonnegotiable, to the extent that we are willing to have our hands branded in the fire for them? "Every one his own truth" in practice does not work. It means, simply, "Don't bother me." It is a form of indifference. It is more honest for a man to contend with the truth than to cravenly surrender to mere tolerance. What credit does it do to a man when we do not try to persuade another person, or when we close our minds to another's attempt to persuade us? Then we live like isolated monads next to each other, and then we engage with each other only in practical matters. With these escape routes, truth no longer corresponds to reality but is a narcotic.

Continuing a discussion concerning truth, we could also look exclusively in the direction of learning. Truth then becomes that which can be demonstrated through pure science. In fact, science has everything to do with truth. Science, after all, is a segment of reality. It is a systematic effort to probe ever more deeply into reality. That appears difficult enough, and the true scientist knows that what we know is only a shell in the ocean of not-knowing. Science is a domain with boundaries. It is not the mandate of science to deal with falsity or to clarify irrelevance in areas not subject to demonstration. Whoever tries that is not a scientist but is entering the arena of faith.

We all know intuitively that the scientific model is impersonal. It does not provide us with life. Truth has to do with the heart. With life. You do not marry as a professor, neither do you die as a professor, but as a human being. And that is just the point of truth. It is about how you relate toward your fellow man, how you get on with your kin, how you live as man, or woman, or how you face death. You can say a hundred times that truth is a word that belongs in the scientific domain, but at the level of *common sense*, this does not ring true. And what does not become internalized is not true.

Can Truth Be Defined?

So, what, then, is truth? A definitive account of truth is not very helpful. That requires us to make distinctions, such as truth *about* things and truth about the *expression* or judgment of things. In this we are not aligned altogether with the idea of this book. It is not that truth is so vague that we cannot compile an account of it very well. Here is the matter. Truth is so very original, so primal, that a definition would obscure more than it would elucidate. Truth has to concern itself with the light that streams from things and people, at its deepest level, not covered over by a veil of commonplaces or a thick blanket of indifference. It refers to the appearance of meaning of life as it was intended, no longer corrupted and concealed. It requires that we must become insiders as we seek to discover these secrets and to reveal the things we wish to open up to daylight. Truth is a life in truth. Truth, therefore, is intimately bound up with the right relationship to yourself and your neighbor, with saying what must be said, and doing what you must do. It is a life that is "transparent to God": it is a witness of yourself and your existence in the light of God and through it into life.

Truth, as I have pointed out above, is a happening. Truth is something which discloses itself, whatever comes to the light. It comes often in the break of the daily routine, often as an insight into what had been concealed or had been shoved under the table. "There came a light to me"; that happens often with a deep intervention to make a happening.

Truth as a Deathly Pale Child

When the truth reveals itself to me, and when I'm beginning to see the light, this means that I have lost that truth. It does, in fact, seem so. In many cases, the truth is the return of truth. That discovery can be a shocking experience. But I have permitted myself to join others swimming easily with the current. I have hardened myself to accept a worldview that suits me the best. I have been seeking a good and worthy ideal, but in pursuing that ideal in this context, I have become hardened, pitiless, and ready even to step on corpses. I have become a professor, have taken on titles, have become a celebrity, have received support from my theories. One day, however, the

Truth, as a beggar, stood at my door and knocked. I have become a respectable citizen, have injured no one, I have shoveled the snow away from the sidewalk of my neighbor, I have remained humble, good to my children. There came a moment, however, when I confronted the truth as if it were a deathly pale child standing outside the door of my life. Outside the door.

King Lear, in the Shakespeare play by that name, has always lived comfortably, surrounded by luxuries of the palace, and has always lent his ear to the palaver of flatterers. This king is brought up short one night—in a night of rain, of darkness, naked and unsheltered, alone, solitary. His eyes are opened to the misery of his fellowmen, the world of these creatures:

> Poor naked wretches, wheresoe'er you are
> That bide the pelting of this pitiless storm,
> How shall your houseless heads and unfed sides
> Your looped and windowed raggedness defend you
> From seasons such as these? O I have ta'en
> too little care of this. Take physic, pomp,
> Expose thyself to feel what wretches feel,
> That thou mayst shake the superflux to them
> And show the heavens more just. (III, 428 ff.)

Truth requires conversion to the truth. The voice of truth, however, has been silenced. And, yet, it is never suppressed entirely. The conscience can be seared with a branding iron, but it cannot be destroyed. Truth has an affinity with reality; it clings to our very existence, and lets itself be heard in unexpected moments.

Truth as Incarnated

Truth can return from unrecognizable sources. Christian faith has heard the voice of truth loudly and clearly in Jesus Christ. This does not imply there is no additional truth. How fortunate we are, having encountered truth in the least expected places. It is always the case that reality itself is based on truth and reflects truth. We encounter truth in our everyday lives, in exploring life's meaning, in philosophy, in religion, and elsewhere.

Still, the truth is continually obscured. It is necessary that we trace it back to its original sources, and in such a way that it has a liberating effect. We hear Jesus say to Pilate, "For this was I born; for this I came into the world, and all who are not deaf to truth listen to my voice" (John 18:37). Elsewhere, Jesus claims to be truth itself (John 14:6).

In all of this, it becomes clear that truth is not merely a set of laws or norms. They do serve as guidelines for our lives, of course—how we must live, what we must do, what we must not do. But despite their efforts to penetrate our hearts in search of truth, they cannot open our hearts to its source. They are, therefore, powerless, and where they are strictly applied, they afflict men with the virus of pride or self-sufficiency. The law shatters in pieces all human imperfection. Nor does truth exist by itself in wise sayings. These gleanings can help, but they do not bring about renewal.

Truth resides ultimately as a person, the person of Jesus Christ. He comes out of the very heart of God. He is the truth of God who presents himself in love for lost mankind and a lost creation. This truth is a life; it is a life that speaks as it silences, that lights up the darkness, that makes whole while being broken itself. Through Jesus, existence is "transparent to God." How lost the world is becomes clear as we see Jesus testify to the truth, alone and abandoned, discovered on a cross. So false has life become. At the same time, the cross represents God's breaking through of truth from the God of love, from his faithfulness and righteousness. ". . . And the truth shall make you free" (John 8:32). That is how the truth functions: deliverance from the lie, the indifferent, spiritual blindness, the self-sufficient. It is the experience of mankind over the centuries that this happens wherever the name of Jesus is heard.

And as this living truth streams into a person, it has potential for growth. "Abide in me," says Jesus. Bathe the truth in baptismal water. Drink the truth in with the wine from the kingdom. So we come into the truth. We come into the truth through a deeper bonding with Jesus. That is how we arrive at the source of truth, from which all truth, and from whom all truth in the world, is derived. That is how truth comes to us.

Attempting to Live in the Truth

Living in the truth is living in close union with the source of truth. It is a life that rouses us from sleep, that wakens us in order to understand the significance of things. It is a life that awakens us to help us see what we have seen for so many years but have not really seen, to listen to hear the voice of a child that was so often expressed but which we have not really heard.

Living in the truth is not a simple matter. It is not easy to let things have their say, to do the right thing to your neighbor, to live with integrity. The power of the lie is strong. Self-interest, indifference, love of ease, lust for power, and whatever else lacks clarity contributes to the silencing of truth. Life is always lived in occupied territory, and we are continually tempted to keep truth at arm's length. Let him that stands, take heed lest he fall. Truth can abide in us only when we remain united with him, and, therefore, let him speak to us. It abides in us when we want to be called from the valleys of death. It abides in us whenever we let ourselves be awakened, if necessary, with a "kyrie eleison" on our lips. Living in the truth is a daunting task, a "Versuch in de Wahreit zu Leben."[1] It is a pilgrimage of falling and getting up. The lowly of heart make the furthest progress on this road while they realize, at the same time, that they have just begun the journey.

Life in the truth is, above all, growth in wisdom. It is not so much a matter of obeying rules. A wise man opens up his heart to reality. He sees through appearances, also in himself. He sees farther than his nose is long. He knows where wisdom comes from and develops a heightened sensitivity. He sees all things *sub specie aeternum*.

Wisdom is not only theoretical; it is also practical. It is precisely by acting that we encounter fractures in reality, but we also learn through these breaks how to avoid perpetuating them. Theoretical truthfulness by itself can easily lead to cynicism or cheap criticism. To live in the truth is to be ready to put your hand to the plow, even though you probably plough but a small part of the acre. It is better that you plough that small plot than that you fail to stretch out your hand.

Triumph of Truth

There will come a time when truth in its entirety will open up to the man who attempts to live in the truth. There will come a time when truth is victorious, when the knowledge of God will cover the earth as the waters cover the sea (Isa 11:9). Then all reality will be transparent to God. The liars will perish forever in the pool of fire.

All of this will come to pass through a painful process, through a time of judgment. Then truth will become distinguished from falsity. Then all generations of mankind who embraced the truth and persevered in it will be separated from those who have drunk from the cisterns of the lie. A huge *catharsis* will take place, an enormous purification, in which all that is true will be brought together. The yearning of creation about which Paul speaks will be fulfilled in that moment. And all this will occur not with

---

1. See Havel, *Versuch in der Wahrheit zu Leben*.

sword or cannon, nor through the enthusiasm of fanatics who take up swords in the name of truth, nor the accumulation of all good intentions or the joint efforts of all idealists. All this will occur because the kingdom has been given to him who stood before Pilate, the rejected one from Nazareth who, nevertheless, testified to the truth.

Then the truth will triumph, along with the right. Also, without its knowledge, history is on the way to the disclosure of truth. History is obviously the history of lies, in small and in great. The lie and unrighteousness gorge on and corrupt everything they touch of reality. Honest speech and discovery of truth accomplish very little against them. The limbo of forgotten things is a complete record of misdeeds and lies committed, from generation to generation, from culture to culture.

And yet this world is intended for the truth, and truth will win the day. Then all things will fall into place. Then the light of God will penetrate all things. Then our lives, too, will be baptized into the light of God. Then the fire of judgment will consume all the lies, so that a higher, purer song of praise will come into being. That side will prevail. Reality is the truth. Truth will have the last word.

3

Goodness

Abounding Generosity

GOODNESS, JUST AS TRUTH, is a distinguishing mark of reality. And just as no satisfactory definition of truth can be given, this is all the more true for goodness. Like truth, it is a word involving origins, a primal word, and, thus, can be defined only by itself. Goodness is best described in company with such ideas as overflowing, with the suggestion of beyond measure, a sea surging on to the shore, a well that modestly and unobtrusively remains running and provides water to a thirsty land, the starry heavens with glistening lights beyond counting as they quietly and inaudibly glide through the heavens all night long.

Goodness comes to us in the breasts from which a baby nourishes herself, in the early and late rains, in the light that thrusts itself upon us every morning. Goodness comes to us in the earth with its riches, the earth that gives seed to the sower and bread to the reaper. Goodness is the light which makes life possible. Life, and "being," are, in themselves, good. It is good that there is "being." All creatures are, as creatures, good, because it is good that they exist and because it is better that they exist than that they do not. It is good because all human beings are one (as it is written, it is not good that man should be alone).

Reality comes forth from the eternal goodness of God, who is goodness itself. Everything that is, proceeds from God, and from the lap of goodness reality will one day be safely restored again. Through the whole of creation, therefore, from all times and all places, songs of praise rise up to the goodness of God, from high in the heavens in the song of the lark to the depths of the sea in the bass of the whale.

Goodness and Freedom

In the world of reality, God has created an open space which provides room for free beings. Man faces the choice whether to remain in that goodness. "Das Güte ist die Freiheit."[1] The goodness of God ranges over all his creatures as gifts which the unfathomable depths have received from freedom.

Freedom is the most distinguishing mark of human beings. Freedom is no mere neutral freedom of choice. Man has not been tossed into this world to oscillate between two choices, as was the famous case of the donkey of Buridan, who was compelled to choose between two identical haystacks, of equal height, the left or the right.

The gift of freedom is not that merciless. Man has the freedom to accept and remain in the good given to him. It is the freedom to want to be himself as a child of the light and of the grace of God. It is the freedom to desire God's world and God himself as is source. It is the freedom to respond to love with love. It is the choice not to desire another world but to affirm this one.

That Yes word is not inconsequential. Will there be a being who will assent to what God declared, that what he saw in the beginning was very good? Will there be a being who will return God's Yes with his own Yes, freely given? Is there to exist a being who acknowledges God's Yes word with joy and lives with a Yes to God? It was a daring moment when God determined out of his goodness that there would be a creature who would be free to make his own judgments and exercise his own free will. And that man was to know that God's goodness is not just a matter of expressing itself in always new creations, but also a matter of practicing restraint, of a pause and a boundary, that makes space for the freedom of another. Will man, built not from a rib, but from the heart of God, say Yes to God, and be willing to be his bride? The cosmos holds its breath. The angels hold their breath. God holds his breath. Then the bridge collapses. The man does something more mysterious than the "gift" of his freedom. He abuses that freedom. He peers into the abyss of his own freedom and falls into it.

---

1. Kierkegaard, *Der Bergriff der Angst*, 573.

And the world collapses. What, now, is all the goodness for? What would happen if the being shown grace would not return this goodness but let it disappear into the abyss of the nothing, the nihilism which is the alternative of goodness? Is goodness destroyed by all this? No. The world remains full of goodness. But there does fall a shadow now over this world. A small shadow, so it appears, a hitch. A No. But this shadow keeps growing and, as a suffocating blanket, seems to stifle goodness.

Goodness Rescued

Does God build upon castles in the sky? Is his experiment with goodness a failed experiment? God had no need of it, really. He was not one who from eternity was looking for a wife. God is not a lonely God longing for friendship. God is fullness itself, a more than one, yes, even a Trinity. The world was not built out of a divine shortage, but out of a divine opulence. Still, it seems as if these boundaries have been crossed. The world is a leaking vessel from which the goodness of God leaks out into a black nothing. Who says the good forces will overcome? Who says that the remaining good will offset the sea of misery and evil which sweeps over this world like a flood?

These questions can be answered only by God himself. It is too huge a question for us. But God answers his own question and gives us an insight into his answer. The world is a leaking vessel, but God does not write it off peremptorily. Goodness keeps streaming in, each century, each year, each day. The tree in front of our house bloomed again in spring. Again, there was the hushed voice in a room from a family in a lower-class neighborhood, for a child had been born to them. Again, people come together to humbly share bread with each other. We find even in the heart of terror a comforting hand, a laugh, a waving greeting over all this barbed wire.

And more than that. God himself streams in. That is a process, a history, a story, a long story. There is not much more to say about the goodness of God after a fall of man and a deluge. After exactly eleven chapters in the Bible, the book is finished—so it seems, anyway, for, surprisingly, that is the point at which the book really begins. The giver becomes a gift. God walks with small steps, almost inaudible, into this leaking world. In the incarnation. In the flesh. The flesh of a small nation, since God is prepared to make himself small. The flesh of a humble girl from Nazareth, for God can make himself still smaller.

The chariot builder in Wagenberg
was a dwarf.
He was so small that he could be placed
in a crib alongside Jesus.
What would the tiny Jesus say about that?
The tiny Jesus found that space not offensive.
(Duinkerken, *In Wagenberg*)

Even in Israel, God's new garden, the goodness of God spilled away, only to be swept away at Golgotha, so it seemed. But Golgotha marks the big turnaround. It appears that at Golgotha God built his goodness on a Yes word which he uttered on the cross. That word rose out of the heart of darkness. The goodness of God encounters a response so powerful, so convincing, that from the death of the old world a new one was being born. It is on the basis of this Yes word that God has wanted the world, and on that Yes word he also grounded it. We live by this word: As in Adam all die, so in Christ will all be brought to life (1 Cor 15:22).

It is not surprising that the goodness of God now takes on the color of red: color of blood, color of wine, color of the red sun after a dark night. The hymn about the goodness of God will always have as its refrain the Lamb of God.

Goodness Endures

Goodness continues to well up also in a world where goodness is violated, scorned, and murdered. The negative forces have great power. They are like a whirlpool pulling down entire generations. The hymn of goodness can fall prey to cynicism and hard-heartedness. And still it gets sung. And still the word of Lamentations is true: "The Lord's love is surely not exhausted, nor has his compassion failed; they are new every morning, so great is his constancy" (Lam 3:22–23).

Reality opposes the demolition. It is not because human beings are ultimately good. He who builds his hope on the goodness of man ends up disappointed. There is much good in and toward man, but the often vilified word from the Heidelberg Catechism that man "is prone to all evil" is simply true. The true resistance resides in the will of the Creator, who is also the Re-Creator.

This resistance appears in thousands of ways. There is a limit to how deep it can penetrate, for no matter how deep the valley, life rises up again.

Ultimately, goodness will triumph. The power of goodness is the power of God whose goodness reaches even to the abyss of the void. God's goodness is present at the beginning and is present at the end. Man will no longer live among ruins, but he will participate in this goodness.

This participation in goodness is a participation in God himself. It is impossible to suppose that one could enjoy God's gifts but not God himself. Man is the creature who may know the Giver of the gifts. In the gifts, God gives himself.

Goodness and the Good Life

Goodness is not only a gift; it is also a life. There *is* such a thing as "a good life." There is no one who does not wish to live a good life. Even the thief and murderer desire such. No one can live a good life without a right judgment of one or another good. That is true because we do not fetch goodness from within ourselves. He who wishes only to be a good person lives in an unreal world. We must therefore be right about our judgment of some good in order to lead a good life. One cannot live a good life, therefore, only in avoidance and prevention. You must not murder (negative) because you have been called to love your neighbor (positive). The judgment that a thing is good implies that we ourselves receive that good and that we continue to cherish, promote, uphold, and love that good.

Not every focus on a good results in a good life. Health is a good, but he who will not risk it to save a drowning child is not a good person. Having the right weight is also a good, but he who busies himself all day long with lifting weights misses the purpose of life. There is a hierarchy of goods. Good gifts can be misused or lead to misuse. They can end up in the wake of egotism, or pride. We need to be converted from egotism or pride, but that conversion must show itself in the substitution of another good.

The highest good must be the weightiest. The highest good is God himself. For that reason Jesus said that we must love God above all else. God gives himself to us in love and, therefore, a good life is a life that receives God's love and responds to him with love. We are directed toward this greatest good. The second good, entwined with the first, is the neighbor. We cannot live without receiving love from the neighbor, and we are likewise enjoined to love our neighbor as ourselves. That love is not just a feeling of one kind or another, but receives shape and form in a life of service and dedication. That is what a good life is all about.

There are more good things. A good life also consists of a commitment to everything that is good. A good life is a life in which one focuses on a positive aspect of this reality in order to get to know it, develop it, and cherish it. Actually, there are innumerable things that are good and ask for our attention.

There are good things that are, however, dangerous and have a dubious side to them. The good that is the most dangerous is money. Money is necessary for life, but it is in itself not a good. Money exercises a dangerous power. Money is an idol. He who lives only to make money from money gets entangled in it and ultimately swerves away from the true good. You cannot love God and mammon. The words are Jesus'.

The Triumph of Goodness

We live in a world of ambiguities. We know of no other world. There is a power of goodness that contests with the power of evil. It often happens that the good turns up right when it is confronted with the evil. So it is not just a hypothetical question whether a world with only good in it would be a livable world. We can't imagine the possibility. A book with only good in it gets to be boring already on page three. We cannot bring such a world into being. There is a book of three parts, Dante's *Divine Comedy*, in which Dante makes an effort in the third part to intimate what a world of all goodness would be like. He is the poet who has come closest to doing so. But for understandable reasons, this is the least popular division of his work. In a world in which you cannot think evil away, a book of sheer goodness is bound to be a poor representation of paradise.

We cannot, indeed, think evil away. That is why, literally speaking, we should not try it either. Just this, when we say that a future world is unthinkable without it, we stand out as a ridiculous figure. What do we know about it? Let us not, then, make ourselves ridiculous, but live in hope. Evil is evil, and if there ever should come a time that it definitely has to give way to the superior power of the good, then all we can do is look forward to that time with deep yearning. Above all, the true good is God himself. Of the good without God we receive enough. Therefore we need not speculate about eternity. Of God himself we can never receive enough. That is precisely what eternity is for.

4

Beauty

Essential Beauty

BEAUTY HAS ALL THE credentials for membership in the Big Three. We are not talking now about some frill or disk or something decorative. Beauty is an identifying mark of reality, just as it is for truth and goodness. Beauty has to do with form and emanation, with shape and charisma. There is something that gets expressed in language, or through the body, a shape. This something insinuates itself into form and gives luster and grace; it searches for an eye, an ear, a heart. This something can also be a person. Beauty is the outward expression of something into something, from a person to something. This is not a definition of beauty. The secret of beauty is not to be hunted down any more than are the secrets of truth and goodness.

There are world views that assign little importance to beauty. If reality is perceived high-handedly as primal soup, then beauty is in that case no longer an expression of something. Then there is only matter, in blind forms, devoid of spirit or soul. On the other hand, idealists such as Descartes do recognize an "I" or soul, but that is stripped of the body. Material, according to Descartes, is extension. He removes from it color, fragrance, and sound. Beauty, then, consists, at most, of something in the human spirit, but it no longer has a basis in reality. Even Plato denigrates beauty now and then as something second best; behind the forms there resides a spirit without a physical form. The body is mere appearance. Fortunately, Plato, such a great and wise thinker, was content to let things rest there.

Without beauty, neither goodness nor truth would have any power of attraction. If goodness were without beauty, a person faced with the choice between good and evil would have no good reason to choose the good. Also, truth without beauty would shrivel up into a hard legalism or un-contestable right. The three, therefore, belong together and pull each other down as they fall. Beauty is the expression of truth and goodness.

On the other hand, beauty without truth and goodness would be only an empty husk with a treacherous power capable of deception.

Genuine beauty appeals to the listener or observer. It calls upon him to change. Consider Rilke's observation in a poem about the Greek sculp-ture of the torso of Apollo:

> . . . denn da ist keine Stelle
> Die dich nicht sieht. Du must dein Leben ändern.
> . . . for here there is no place
> that does not see you. You [observer] must change your life.

Beauty speaks to the listener. It appeals not only to an aesthetic emo-tion but also implies a moral meaning. It is something which is good and something which is true that radiates from the torso of Apollo. It addresses us. Goodness and truth enjoin you to change your life, almost by definition, because it is given a form that cannot be distinguished from the contents.

It appears, according to Rilke's rule, that what is present is not only a form and radiation, but also an observer, someone who contemplates whenever the subject is beauty. Of what use is art if it does not meet the eye or ear? Perhaps "Observation" is still too weak. "You must change your life." Beauty stirs not alone the eye, but the heart as well, and the will. It shakes things up; it tugs at us, it sets things in motion, it prompts a response, and devotion. It takes you out of yourself. Form and expression respond with observation, love, sight, and devotion. And love.

Beauty in the Life of Nature

Many folk equate beauty with nature. No matter what, nature still basks in the afterglow of paradise. Or is that a prelude to an ending? Those who let Psalm 104 speak to them can surmise from it that ancient Israel also looked at nature—as creation.

That view is not universally accepted. Sometimes it appears as if creation has been struck dead and flattened, that it has become ugly and lifeless, grubby and dirty. Sometimes it can happen that nature looks at us as a sphinx, with a deceitful eye. Sometimes nature alters its appearance and hides itself, withdrawing itself from the looks of the observer. On the other hand, nature sometimes tempts man to view it as divine, compelling him to bow on his knees and thereby commit treason at the deepest level of his being.

> But sometimes it happens that the breath of God moves over his whole creation: It has seemed to me sometimes as though the Lord breathes on this poor gray ember of Creation and it turns to radiance—for a moment or a year or the span of life. And then it sinks back into itself again, and to look at it no one would know it had anything to do with fire, or light . . . Wherever you turn your eyes the world can shine like transfiguration. You don't have to bring a thing to it except a little willingness to see it. Only, who could have the courage to see it?[1]

All we need is some willingness to see it. For that you don't have to go to Switzerland for a vacation. The experience can happen in your own back yard, where a tree stands, from early spring to late winter.

Much of Romantic poetry is for the greatest part an effort to view nature as animated. Decadence characterizes much of this "aestheticism," this ideology of "art for art's sake," but, at its best, this poetry still appeals to the imagination. I am convinced that the notion of an inspired nature can ultimately be maintained only through a faith in the Creator. Again, "It seems to me sometimes as though the Lord breathes on this poor gray ember of Creation," and by this it lights up creation.

No one is forced to accept this belief, and, fortunately, the beauty of creation strikes many a person in an unguarded moment, in the blink of an eye, and there are people who have had "a little willingness to see it." Beauty is more than a play of forms, more also than the subjective perception of an observer. It is the expression where soul and spirit are prompted to work together, a relationship which stands or falls with a Spirit which makes everything possible.

1. Robinson, *Gilead*, 279.

Beauty in the Human Being

God appears in the garments of nature and in the sign language of history. For that reason it is also possible for the human being to assert himself. A flower does that. An animal does that. And, above all, man can do that. The glory of God radiates over man. The man is an "image of God," and what else can that mean than that man may also express himself?

Man is a spirit and body, a soul and form. There is an ambience of the soul which manifests itself in a form. Must we really abolish that? No. The spirit exists, although never approachable as such; nor is it easy to find. And yet the spirit exists and is sometimes even palpable. Listen once more to Marilynne Robinson:

> By "life" I mean something like "energy" (as the scientists use the word) or "vitality," and also something very different. When people come to speak to me, whatever they say, I am struck by a kind of incandescence in them, the "I" whose predicate can be "love" or "fear" or "want," and whose object can be "someone" or "nothing" and it won't really matter, because the loveliness is just in that presence, shaped around "I" like a flame on a wick, emanating itself in grief and guilt and joy and whatever else. But quick, and avid, and resourceful. To see that aspect of life is a privilege of the ministry which is seldom mentioned.[2]

The "I" in that fragment is not naked, but an "I" who radiates presence. That is the wonder of a living "I." That is an indefinable but yet real kernel. The great English poet Hopkins wrote about the "instress" or "inscape" of things in the person, the unique combination of energies which constitutes the uniqueness of this particular individual. The secret of reality lies in the "instress," the "I-ness," or "thisness" and not in one uniform primal matter. This "instress" displays itself, can be guessed, comes to expression, finds space to fashion forms. There is a body, a clanking sound. And many "I's" assemble themselves together to make a greater whole. Two in the marriage. Three in the family. One hundred in community.

What must the Creator be like who, with an inexhaustible overflow of gifts, endows everything with a "this-ness," and to fill the world with them? The Creator does not restrict himself with respect to numbers or uniformity. He *does* revel in things "counter, original, spare and strange" (Hopkins), all of them glowing kernels, and all with their own garments.

2. Ibid, 51.

The Beauty of the Transcendental

Many people live in tension concerning the disparity between faith and beauty. What does Christ have to do with beauty? And God himself? The revelation of God is Word, a summons not to see and yet believe.

And, indeed, those who with a preconceived opinion about beauty and culture, who enter the world of faith and revelation, of God and Christ, will drop out disappointed. However, it is more likely that many have adopted the ideals of beauty and culture in the place of faith. Many people now tend to nature and art who formerly adhered to religion and faith. Rather nature than the supernatural, rather art than anything cultus, rather the muse than Mary, rather Apollo than Christ, rather aesthetics than religion, rather the church of "uncarved wood" than the church of wood and stone.

This is not the place to elaborate on these shifting priorities. However, the question should be asked honestly to what extent beauty has not been put outside the door of the Christian tradition. It appears sometimes that prizes are being awarded for ugliness. There are church buildings that are ripe for the landfill. But not only church buildings. I am thinking of Protestant tastelessness where in the name of "the word" no appeal is made to the imagination. I think of Roman Catholic kitsch where nothing gets said. I think of stern moralism, shriveled biblicism, rigid dogmatism, and calcified piety.

I do not intend all this to be a simplistic plea for polished forms and beautiful music in the worship service. Nor is it a protest against sensible religious doctrine or dogmatics. Nor will I say that God is just another word for a quiet moment alongside a pleasant happening or a rewarding event. As concerns that last point, God is God, and faith in God involves death and resurrection, or everything would be about nothing.

For all that, the better contemporary art veers away from this sort of simplicity. It is more the pseudo-theologians that fall into this trap. It is about discovering a beauty in the revelation of God that is not brought in from the outside but arises from that revelation itself. That can happen only when God himself expresses himself. God as the true God makes himself known, and God as the All-Good one makes himself known, and God as the benevolent God reveals himself. He does that through the resources of nature and the Bible, through the means of signs and sacraments. He does that as well through the revelation above all revelations: Christ. Right there, in those shapes of this God, the deepest beauty of God lies concealed.[3]

I point out in this connection the relevance of the Hebrew word *kabod* and the Greek word *doxa* in the Bible. The kabod is the radiating light in which God appears. God appears as the glorious One. "The Lord made the heavens. Majesty and glory attend him" (Ps 96:5, 6). Isaiah sees God seated on the throne in the temple and, above him, the seraphs. God is as the holy one the *mysterium tremendum*, the fear-inspiring mystery, but also the *mysterium fascinans,* the secrecy that attracts (Rudolf Otto, *Het heilige*). And of Christ it was said, "And we beheld his glory" (John 1:14). The glory shows forth in the words and deeds of the Lord. There are moments when this glory crashes through, as when the heavens open above Christ. The transfiguration on the mountain is the most concentrated of such moments. "And in their presence he was transfigured; his clothes became dazzling white, with a whiteness no bleacher on earth could equal" (Mark 9:2–3).

The glory deepens at the cross. It appears to be the end of all glory. But what sort of glory is it that hangs in a reddish cloud and does not show up in darkness and the abyss? It was on a hostile Golgotha that the glory of an exceedingly merciful God appeared. It was a glory that said more than the earlier one did, "You must change your life." But it is also the glory of the bridegroom who says, "I love you." Everything gets relinquished at the foot of the cross—ideals, glorious dreams, and world views. But at the same time it is exactly here that the beauty of love and truth are revealed in a manner that attracts hearts and moves lives. It is no one less than the prince of glory who died on the cross:

> See from His head, His hands, His feet,
> Sorrow and love flow mingled down!
> Did e'er such love and sorrow meet,
> Or thorns compose so rich a crown?
> His dying crimson, like a robe
> Spreads o'er His body on the tree;
> Then I am dead to all the globe,
> And all the globe is dead to me.
> (John Wesley, "When I Survey the Wondrous Cross")

The book Song of Songs is the book which supplies the language for this reality. It is language of shape and grace; it is language of bride and bridegroom, of love and eros. This language will endure to death; indeed,

3. Hamann, "Aesthetica in nuce," 343.

precisely in and through death it receives new meaning. Were this language to disappear, the Christian faith would become a matter of principles and dogma, a body of morality, an ideal. Such an event would no longer stir the heart and touch the soul. No abounding grace any more, and no surrender, but a creaking system, a vague ideal and a gloomy compulsion.

The center of sacred history is a love story, a narrative of a bride and a bridegroom. God comes to us not as an abstract spirit, not with a lashing command, but as God, and, therefore, as beauty, so old and so new. That is how Augustine understood it:

> Too late have I loved you. O you Beauty of ancient days, yet ever new . . . You called, shouted, and burst my deafness. You flashed, shone and scattered my blindness. You breathed out wondrous odors. Finally I drew in my breath and craved your aroma. I tasted until I knew hunger and thirst. You touched me, and I burned for your peace.[4]

This narrative can never be fixed. And Protestants never weary of saying that faith comes from hearing. But what word is being heard? What other than the voice which says, "Behold, I make all things new"? That is an eye-opener. God comes to us and touches what lies in our hearts and minds, and, also, if what is there is more spiritual than physical in nature. God is not a cold faith object. He is "bliss, unspeakable."

Beauty and Criticism

The history of God and man is about how to restore this image. To put it another way: the bride must be made beautiful. It is true, the church has often become a whore, but the poor are those who no longer see the bride. To be sure, it is said a man is only a junction of an invisible play of genes, derived seemingly from nowhere. But he who reduces life to a complex of genes is ignorant of what man is. As the breath of God moves over mankind, the men are as gray cinders which start glowing.

Criticism is essential. Analysis is useful. A dissection knife may be necessary. Sometimes to penetrate appearances. Sometimes in order to give room to our eagerness to investigate. Sometimes because a habit becomes stale. The bronze serpent, a symbol of rescue, must in certain moments be

4. Augustine, *Confessions*, Book 10, XXVII, 38.

broken into pieces. Iconoclasts roar as a scourge throughout the history of the church and Christendom in order to clear the way for the Spirit.

Criticism, however, can also be destructive. Reality then is struck lifeless, and creation is reduced to chemistry. But does that mean that the end of all wisdom is the ugly, the gray, and the everyday life stuff? In the good book we read that the fear (and fascination) of the Lord is the beginning of wisdom. That provides another way of looking at it—deeper and more gracious. The world will not perish because of ugliness because the Lord is determined to let his glory shine upon and in the objects. Those who pluck the flowers in order to analyze the stem will never be attracted to the flower.

In Conclusion

If Christ rescues the "I-ness" and "thisness," it is no great wonder that he himself appears in the way of all that lives and moves. Beauty receives a new sound. Beauty's color resembles that of Christ. By way of conclusion, both to this section and to this book, I give you the word of Hopkins, probably the most beautiful poem he wrote:

The Windhover
To Christ our Lord

I caught this morning morning's minion,

kingdom of daylights's dauphin, dapple-dawn-drawn Falcon, in his riding

Of the rolling level underneath him steady air, and striding

High there, how he rung upon the rein of a wimpling wing

In his ecstasy! then off, off forth on swing,

As a skate's heel sweeps smooth on a bow-bend: the hurl and gliding

Rebuffed the big wind. My heart in hiding

Stirred for a bird,—the achieve of, the mastery of the thing!

Brute beauty and valour and act, oh, air, pride, plume, here Buckle!

AND the fire that breaks from thee then, a billion Times told lovelier,

more dangerous, O my chevalier!

No wonder of it: sheer plod makes plough down sillion

Shine, and blue-bleak embers, ah my dear

Fall, gall themselves, and gash gold-vermillion.

Beauty in the flight of a falcon. Beauty between diving and breaking out. Reality is beautiful. And hidden in and through it all, we see the Lord of creation. Riding on the wind. Throwing off light as he breaks through. Praise him.

Bibliography

Achterberg, Gerrit. *Verzamelde Gedichten* [Selected poems]. Amsterdam: Querido's Uitgeverij, 1964.

Augustine. *Selected Writings of St. Augustine.* Edited by Roger Hazelton. Cleveland: World, 1962.

Balthasar, Hans Urs von. *Theodramatik.* German ed. Vols. 1–4. Einsiedeln, Germany: Johannes Verlag, 1973.

Beckett, Samuel. *Waiting for Godot.* New York: Grove, 1982.

Blake, William. *The Poetry and Prose of William Blake.* Edited by David V. Erdman. Garden City: Doubleday, 1965.

Boer, Theo. "Kunnen Protestanten zonder de Biecht [Can Protestants do without confession]?" In *Een Lichte Last: Protestantse Over de Kerk* [A light burden: Protestant theologians about the church], edited by Gerrit de Kruijf and Witske de Jong, 250–68. Zoetermeer, Netherlands, 2010.

Chesterton, G. K. *Orthodoxy.* New York: Doubleday, 1910.

Coleridge, Samuel Taylor. *The Rime of the Ancient Mariner.* New York: Potter, 1965.

Dostoyevski, Fyodor. *Crime and Punishment.* Translated by Constance Garnett. New York: Dodd & Mead, 1963.

Duinkerken, Anton van. *In Wagenberg.* In *Verzamelde Geschriften: Vertelling en Vertoog.* Antwerp: Uitgeverij: Het Spectrum, 1962.

Eliot, T. S. *The Complete Poems and Plays.* New York: Harcourt, Brace, 1952.

Gunning, J. H., Jr. "Voorbede." In *Goed van God Denken: Teksten uit Magdalena* [Thinking well about God: Texts from Magdalena], 25–34. An almanac yearbook, 1858–1890. Zoetermeer: Boekencentrum, 2010.

Hamann, Johann Georg. "Aesthetica in Nuce." In *Johann Georg Hamann: Eine Auswahl aus seinen Schriften* [A selection from his writings], edited by Martin Seils, 315–54. Wuppertal, Germany: Brockhaus, 1987.

Hauerwas, Stanley. *Working with Words: On Learning to Speak Christian.* Eugene, OR: Cascade, 2011.

Havel, Vaclav. *Versuch in der Wahrheit zu Leben* [Searching for truth in life]. Hamburg: Rowohlt, 1990.

Hofmannsthal, Hugo von. "Das Salzburger Welttheater." In *Gesammelte Werken, Dramen*, vol. 3. Frankfurt am Main, Germany: 1957.

Hopkins, Gerard Manley. *A Selection of His Poems and Plays*. Baltimore, Maryland: Penguin, 1956.

Huizinga, Johan. *The Waning of the Middle Ages*. New York: St. Martin's, 1984.

John of the Cross. *Donkere nacht* [Dark night (of the soul)]. Nijmegen, Netherlands: SUN, 2001.

Kierkegaard, Søren. "Das Buch Adler." In *Einübung im Christentum und anderes*, 483. Translated from the Danish original. Munich: Deutscher Taschenbuch, 1977.

———. *Der Bergriff der Angst* [The concept of anxiety]. Translated by Howard V. Hong and Edna H. J. Hong. Princeton: Princeton University Press, 1980.

———. *Die Krankheit zum Tode* [The sickness unto death]. Munich: Deutscher Taschenbuch, 1976.

Liedboek voor de kerken [Songbook of the churches]. Boekencentrum's Gravenhage, 1973.

Mann, Thomas. *Doctor Faustus: Het leven van de Duitse toondichter Adrian Leverkühn* [Doctor Faustus: The life of the German composer, Adrian Leverkühn]. Translated into Dutch by Thomas Graftdijk. Amsterdam: Arbeiderspers, 1985. English edition translated by John E. Woods. Vintage, 1999.

Nietzsche, Friedrich. *Die Fröhliche Wissenschaft* [The gay science]. Munich, 1954. Originally published 1882. Translated into English in *The Portable Nietzsche*, by Walter Kaufmann, 93–102. New York, Viking, 1968.

———. *Thus Spoke Zarathustra*. In *The Portable Nietzsche*, translated by Walter Kaufmann, 103–349. New York: Viking, 1968.

Pascal, Blaise. *Pensées and The Provincial Letters*. New York: Random House, 1941.

Plaisier, Arjan. *Deep Wisdom from Shakespeare's Dramas*. Translated by Steve van der Weele. Eugene, OR: Wipf & Stock, 2012. Originally published in Dutch as *Is Shakespeare ook onder de Profeten?* Zoetermeer, Netherlands: Uitgeverij, Boekencentrum, 2008.

———. *Protestante kerk in Nederland, Spreken over God* [The Protestant Church in the Netherlands: Talking about God]. Zoetermeer, Netherlands: Uitgeverij, Boekencentrum, 2008.

Rilke, Rainer Maria. "Archaïscher Torso Apollos." In *Sämtliche Werke*. Frankfurt am Main: Insel, 1955. English version, "Archaic Torso of Apollo," in *Ahead of All Parting: Selected Poetry and Prose*, translated by Stephen Mitchell. New York: Modern Library, 1995.

Robinson, Marilynne. *Gilead*. London: Virago, 2004.

Shakespeare, William. *King Lear*. Arden ed. Edited by R. A. Foakes. London: Thomson Learning, 1997.

Tolkien, J. R. R. *The Two Towers*. New York: Del Rey, 2012.